From the Shepherd's Staff

–

The Remix:

Words of Impact, Empowerment and Witness for a Challenging World

Dr. Noel G. L. Hutchinson, Jr.

From the Shepherd's Staff - The Remix

RiverHouse Publishing, LLC
1509 Madison Avenue
Memphis, TN 38104

All **RiverHouse, LLC** Titles, Imprints and Distributed Lines are available at special quantity discounts for bulk purchases for sales promotions, premiums, fund-raising and educational or institutional use.

ISBN **978-0-9988108-6-7**

To my helpmeet and greatest supporter—my wife,
Rebecca

In thankfulness and memory of my parents,

Noel G. L. Hutchinson, Sr.
1916-1993
&
Agnes D. Hutchinson
1921-2007

and to the "great cloud of witnesses" that under gird
my steps

Foreword

Foreword to "From the Shepherd's Staff"
Frank A. Thomas

Most recently, at a conference of African American scholars, I asked the question as to why we do not write more. I was responding to my firm conviction that African American scholars, and in this instance, I include pastors, need to write much more. I realize that ours is an oral tradition, and much of the genius of the Black church travels in oral tradition. But there is something to be said for the written word because too much of the genius of the Black church has gone to the grave with our pastors, preachers, and scholars because we did not get much of it to paper. I believe that when we write, we leave a tangible and discernible record. When we write, generations not yet born can interpret and understand how we addressed, responded to, and met the challenges of our day. When we write, we shape and direct our own history, and our identity is not left for others to write, construct, and define. When we write, we name ourselves, and teach our people the ancient tradition of action and reflection – we need reflection to act and action to make our reflection meaningful. It with the firm conviction about the need for African American pastors, preachers, and scholars to write that I am excited to endorse this powerful book, "From the Shepherd's Staff," by Noel G. L. Hutchinson, Jr.

I have known Noel Hutchinson, Jr. for over fifteen years, and in that time he has distinguished himself as a great communicator and critical interpreter of the events of our time with a unique perspective that joins theology and current events. From these weekly contributions of "From the Shepherd's Staff" to his weekly television program, he has sought to unapologetically interpret the events of our times and days through the lens of African American Christianity, or what he calls "Christoafrocentric" thought. Hutchinson sees his responsibility as an undershepherd that helps "congregants, through an understanding of the Bible, be able to interpret and navigate the times in which they live." Many pastors would articulate the same thing, but so few write their reflections down for their people to read and study.

Based upon wise scholarship and deep compassion, Hutchinson addresses the issues of our day, and is, what many churches are criticized for not being, relevant. He is relevant to the needs, issues, concerns of his church community and the community outside the doors of the church. I without hesitation recommend this book to clergy, laity, and anyone who seeks to be relevant to the community that they serve. Hutchinson is a wise man, with wise thoughts that can change the world.

Frank A. Thomas
Professor of Preaching
Christian Theological Seminary
Indianapolis, Indiana

Table of Contents

Endorsements

Rev. Dr. Noel Hutchinson is a man of profound faith who has a deep understanding of the Gospel that he effectively translates so we can better understand our practical walk through life. He brings clarity to the WORD that allows the faithful and even those who might doubt the presence of God to come to terms with the human experience. In a day and age when the very existence of God is called into question, Rev. Dr. Hutchinson is that beacon that allows us to see through the fog of a world consumed by arrogance and greed. I recommend this book as a sanity-check; a down payment on faith that will yield great dividends to those willing to open their hearts and minds to the word of God.

Walter Fields
CEO/Executive Editor
NorthStarNews.com
March 2014

There's an old hymn that reminds us "We've a story to tell to the nations." This collection of life-supporting and humanizing mini-sermonettes builds upon and revives a vital teaching tradition of the great preachers of the Black Church while speaking to the nation and the world about the many ways we can live the gospel in everyday life. The Shepherd's Staff is a christoafrocentric message that empowers its readers to live a

Christianity that builds a more just and gracious world--"a kingdom of love and light."

Cheryl Townsend Gilkes
John D. and Catherine T. MacArthur Professor
African American Studies and Sociology
Director, African American Studies Program
Colby College,
Waterville, Maine

This "read" will challenge your Ideology, Theology and Etiology of culture views, as well as an insight of one of the great minds in the 21st century....

Dr. Ivory L. Taylor Ed.D
CEO, MUTV1
Memphis, Tennessee

There was once a time when the biblical stories were common in our community. They resonated in our homes, schools and workplaces. In fact, many people in the African American community learned to read using the Bible as their primary reader. For better and for worse that is no longer the case making the role of the preacher to translate ancient sacred wisdom in contemporary language so that lives are still transformed by the message of the Gospel. Dr. Noel Hutchinson meets that challenge in the remix of Shepherd's Staff. I recommend it easily to those who still expect the Word of God to be a light and lamp for today's world.

Dr. Rosalyn R Nichols
Pastor of Freedom's Chapel Christian Church
Executive Director,
The Dr. Henry Logan Starks Institute for Faith, Race & Social Justice,
Memphis Theological Seminary
Memphis, Tennessee

Celebratory, bold, triumphant and soberly honest!!! Noel Hutchinson addresses practical issues and profound truths most Christians are afraid to touch in these "politically incorrect "times. With his concise but direct insights, Hutchinson both disturbs and moves us to willingly face the deepest barriers to a Christ-centered hope.

Rev. Anthony Henderson
Pastor, Beulah Baptist Church
Memphis, Tennessee

The **Shepherd's Staff** is a valuable and far too rare theological hermeneutic of current events. It needs to be studied and implemented as praxis in contemporary preaching and informal discussions. It gives us Christian mediations over contemporary happenings.

Dr. Randolph Meade Walker
Pastor, Castalia Baptist Church
Memphis, Tennessee

From the crucible of the Black Church, Noel Hutchinson puts together vignettes that bring together head and heart, the Bible and the newspaper, in a powerful way. This is recommended reading for those who wish to know how to live out the Gospel in real life for real times

Dr. Gina Stewart
Pastor, Christ Missionary Baptist Church
Memphis, Tennessee

The voice of the Shepherd must be clear, the voice of the shepherd must provide correction and most of all the voice of the shepherd must provide comfort. Hutchinson provide God's sheep with these essentials.

Dr. George W.C. Lyons
Pastor, Gillfield Baptist Church
Petersburg, Virginia

From the Shepherd's Staff exemplifies the potential for pastors to raise both the spiritual and social consciousness of our people far beyond the sermon and pulpit. Dr. Hutchinson guides us through the landscapes of life and scripture in ways that make pastoral ministry more righteous and relevant. I am further reminded of the power of the pastor's pen and voice.

Rev. Earle Fisher
Senior Pastor, Abyssinian Baptist Church
Memphis, Tennessee

Noel Hutchinson shapes conversations that deal with what people wrestle with every day, and wraps them in the hope found in the Bible. He creatively gives the reader much food for thought, and all of us are the better for it

Dr. Stacy L. Spencer
Pastor, New Direction Christian Church
President, Memphis Interfaith Coalition of Action and Hope (MICAH)
Memphis, Tennessee

Introduction

A blank computer screen with a blinking cursor would greet me every week. On Monday it softly whispered. On Tuesday the whisper became a medium call; on Wednesday a persistent hum, and on Thursday morning - the day of my self-imposed deadline, a vibrant, loud and persistent tea kettle-like whistle.

I'm not referring to the manuscript or outline of my sermon, which is a different yet persistent challenge. The task I reference, when completed, filled the back of the church bulletin, known at First Baptist Church Lauderdale as *The Herald.* It is a space that is the possession of the pastor to manage as he wills; the church knows this space as "From the Shepherd's Staff." The staff was a primary tool of the ancient shepherd, which could both comfort and corral the sheep. It served as a tool of guidance and protection. The sheep knew that when the staff presented itself, the shepherd was there. "From the Shepherd's Staff" became a way for the pastor to execute this type of presence among the congregation.

Back before internet blogs and other electronic media vehicles, quite a few pastors used the church bulletin to communicate with their congregation. This practice began at First Baptist under the pastorate of Dr. Charles Dinkins, my immediate predecessor. As a young, newly minted pastor, I took my cues on how to initially use the space from him. For the first year it was a struggle, because I never considered myself a writer. Along the way, several encouragers, from the late Dr. Benjamin Hooks and his brother Raymond, to my wife Rebecca, mentors such as Dr. Fred C. Lofton, First Baptist members such as Deacon Aaron A. Powell, Sr., and family members Nadia Hutchinson and Julie Hutchinson, nudged me into the arena of writing books.

Most of what you will read on the following pages are the words of a pastor to his congregants; and because of their broad impact, they extend from the congregation to the community at large. These words made it to paper because there is some subject matter that requires more time for proper and extensive discussion than Sunday morning worship allows. Instead, after thought and mediation, the necessary words find their way into the "Shepherd's Staff."

Part of my role as a pastor - an under shepherd - is to help my congregants, through an understanding of the Bible, to be able to interpret and navigate the times in which they live. Some might say this task is best left to historians or sociologists. I know, based on my conversations with several of my members over the years, that they expected me to have a perspective attached to an understanding of one's Christian witness. Another way of stating this is a common phrase attributed to several theologians that says, "When shaping an understanding of the world, one should have a newspaper in one hand, and a Bible in the other."

As I talk to many people, either through my TV show or in general as a pastor, I see a need for many to discern some credible, thought-out ways to view current events and society through the lens of the Bible instead of the other way around. I agree with Robert McAfee Brown, who in his book, *The Bible Speaks To You*, wrote, "...the minute you take your 'religion' seriously, you've got to be concerned about your fellow men, and in our kind of world concern for fellow men inevitably means concern with the political arena in which men live. Since the 'gospel' is concerned not only with individuals, but with individuals in their social relationships, it must be relevant to the way people order their social relationships in politics and government."[i]

Since the publication of the first edition of this book, I've received nothing but praise. Many appreciated the integration of theology with current events. Others enjoyed the well-thought-out perspectives on critical issues. Yet others, thinking that the conservative evangelical and prosperity gospel viewpoints currently ruling mainstream media was the *only* Christian voice, took the content of the first edition as a breath of fresh air.

Thinking about a follow-up to the initial book, I wrestled with doing a totally new volume. I decided, however, to take a page out of the hip hop genre – which I'm quite familiar with; growing up watching its birth and spread throughout the world. The Merriam Webster dictionary defines a remix as "a new or different version of a recorded song that is made by changing or adding to the original recording of the song." I remember when Mary J. Blige and Method Man did a version of "You're All I Need to Get By," originally done by Marvin Gaye and Tammi Terrell. A music purist might ask, "Why mess with perfection?" The point was to reach a new audience unfamiliar with the original. In their version, you could hear the heartbeat of Black New York, and the flavor of a new generation. Around the same time, in gospel music, Vanessa Bell Armstrong did a new version of "Peace Be Still' so impactful that James Cleveland, the arranger/writer of the original version, used the end of this newer one during live concerts until his death in 1991. In the true, direct spirit of the remix, the R&B group Jagged Edge did a remix of their hit, "Let's Get Married" that kept the vocals but changed the backing music to "It's Like That" by Run DMC and added a cameo rap from Run himself. The remix was a bigger seller, with more impact than the original. Countless reggae artists over the last 30 years have done the same thing with similar success.

Hence, I present to you *From the Shepherd's Staff—The Remix*. It's a remix like that from the legendary Harlem clothier Dapper Dan, who uses luxury goods and their symbols in the remixing of clothes for a new audience.[ii] Just like gumbo, I've taken my cross-genre renderings, whether from the original book, newer entries, Facebook posts, op-ed pieces or press conferences, and mixed them together into a new fit. The vocals are the same—I'm still the singer—but the musical bed has been adjusted for a wider audience. This book can be a catalyst for self-improvement or new engagement in your community. It may be the start of helping you begin a fully shaped relationship with Jesus Christ. It can also push you to engage in deeper study for some of the issues it raises.

What you will read in this book is a particular, unapologetically presented, theological perspective. I'll sum it up in a word you will see elsewhere in this book: Christoafrocentric. It is a word I coined some time ago, which has seen use over the years to describe the synthesis between my faith and the reality of where I live; without compromising either one. What does this mean? I'm a Christian, and my Christian understanding, along with the theological stance that undergirds this book, recognizes that the living of one's witness is done within a particular context. Your context is your community, the culture that you find all around you. It is also the culture out of which a local congregation engages in ministry. First Baptist Church Lauderdale is one of the oldest African-American churches originally within the city borders of Memphis, and is a church steeped in the midst of African-American life. First Baptist is anchored in South Memphis, in one of the most historic blocks of any in the entire African diaspora; sitting yards from the mother church of the Church of God in Christ, and across the street from Booker T. Washington High School – Memphis' first high school for African-Americans. It is a similar context to the one that shaped me as an African-American growing up in The Bronx with some of the same challenges and concerns. In this context, the issues of life must be filtered through the Bible to give the prescription of encouragement in life. As such, my approach, both in ministry and in writing these pieces, always has at its heart the need to give a holistic, comprehensive response.

While reading the various "Shepherd's Staff" pieces included in this volume, bear in mind that the genesis of what you see initially targeted the congregation of First Baptist Church Lauderdale. Most of the entries you see are what the congregation saw, with few changes. Some of these writings made their way into *The Commercial Appeal*, Memphis' daily newspaper, and the *North Star News*, an internet publication that focuses on news from an African-American perspective. In November of 2013, through other conversations prompted by some of the very pieces I'd written for the "Shepherd's Staff," doors were opened for me to do a local television show, *Black Thought*, on MUTV1 (now the M1 network), Memphis' first Black-owned television station. In all of these cases, the catalyst that opened these doors was a pastor communicating with his congregants. Several pieces are centered on news and events that were happening, or had recently happened, at the time they were written. Reading about these incidents now will give an interesting perspective on what took place then. Several more pieces focus on Christian living, while others focus on personal introspection and special events in the life of the church. All of them attempt to put the Bible, the newspaper, and life's challenges together into a comprehensive fit.

The book's first section, "The Bible and You," sets the foundation for the rest of the book; describing the process of having the Bible in one hand and the newspaper in the other. It completes this process by showing how a careful use of Scripture can inform how we interpret the times in which we live. In this section we especially see how, in spite of political persuasion, to use the Biblical lens in assessing how to deal with societal ills.

The next section, "Examples from Everyman/Woman and the Rich & Famous," is a type of requiem, a memorial, for the recently departed of the rich and famous; gleaning from positive examples in their lives. We also look at everyman and everywoman and see how their actions can be emulated. "God and the Holidays" is a look at how we view holidays through the lens of context (where we live) and the Bible, and also presents the concept of Christoafrocentricity.

"Cross-pollination: Conversations Between Various Platforms" acknowledges the impact of social media. Here we view several social media posts along with items from a press conference. In a couple of cases, we will see how musings and critical commentary on Facebook wound up in the local newspaper and television broadcasts. The

Facebook entries are more strident, more "in your face," as this is the nature of social media. Other entries in this section originated on a blog, eventually moving to a "Shepherd's Staff" entry on a subsequent Sunday morning. The nature of technology and social media makes this cross-pollination possible—and necessary. The point is to show the impact of a well-placed, positive word; which can have influence across various platforms.

Three sections follow under the general title of "The Christian Life and You," which deal directly with how to live a Christian witness in the world, looking at several aspects of the average life. "Stony the Road We Trod" specifically looks at occurrences that directly affect African-Americans, with suggested solutions and applications. "Why, God? What is the Answer?" addresses how God interacts with us in life's challenging times. "Family Matters & Personal Reflections: As I See It" is self-explanatory. The next section, "Empowerment 101," covers how you and I can strengthen ourselves through Christ and our own initiative.

The last section is "Miscellaneous—The Parking Lot." In many community meetings, items come up that are important, but fall outside of the agenda. So their impact doesn't get lost, they're written down in a list called "the parking lot" to be addressed later. Here, at the end of the book, are items that didn't make the other sections but are important enough to be a part of this conversation.

In January 2018, after prayerful consideration, I transitioned away from the church I pastored for over 22 years - First Baptist Church Lauderdale - with no animus, to the beginning stages of organizing a new work – Greater Works Fellowship; theologically anchored in John 14:12:

Very truly, I tell you, the one who believes in me will also do the works that I do and, in fact, will do greater works than these (NRSV).

As of this writing it is in the embryonic, organizational stage, and will embody much of the thoughts highlighted in this book. It gives you this book's subtitle—Words of Impact, Empowerment, and Witness for a Challenging World. You can go to www.greaterworksmemphis.com for updates concerning its progress.

As you read this book, may it, in the spirit of the re-mix, empower, enlighten and inspire you. Remember, the musical bed may be different, but the message remains the same. Be blessed.

CHAPTER ONE - THE BIBLE AND YOU

- The Purpose of the Shepherd's Staff and the Church
- The Newspaper and the Bible
- Some Ways the Church is Needed in Our Society
- Our Relationship and Lifestyle
- How Should Christians Critique Current Events?

The Purpose of the Shepherd's Staff and the Church
June 29, 2003

It is my attempt in this space to view life through the lens of Scripture. To put it another way, current events should be viewed with the Bible in one hand and the newspaper in the other. This approach is necessary because our relationship with Jesus is not like a light switch that's toggled on and off at a whim; it is meant to be constantly "on" so that everything is in view. Therefore everything we do and all things around us should be seen from the perspective of an active Christian witness.

From this perspective, the news over the last two weeks has been disturbing. A store manager admits to stealing money and setting a fire to cover up the crime. Two people die as a result. Babies in three different locations are left in vehicles in 90+ degree weather, and all of them die. A woman goes on a marijuana and ecstasy induced drug binge in a club. On the way home she hits a homeless man with her car and leaves him on her windshield to die.

We are a part of the "Black church." This designation is a cultural and social one born in the dark midnight of slavery. Scripture tells us that there is one church—the bride of Christ—a multicultural one. For our conversation today, I refer to that segment of the church known as the Black church, because it, I believe, is the vehicle that will reach many of our people. Jesus said in Matthew 7:3-5, *Why do you look at the speck of sawdust in your brother's eye and pay no attention to the plank in your own eye? How can you say to your brother, "Let me take the speck out of your eye" when all the time there is a plank in your own eye? You hypocrite, first take the plank out of your own eye, and then you will see clearly to remove the speck from your brother's eye.*

We are 140 years removed from the Emancipation Proclamation and the end of slavery. In essence, this is four long generations ago. Some of you who are reading this knew people who were born enslaved. We left this institution without equipment or preparation but with determination. Today many of us have the equipment, but no determination or preparation. We have been told not to blame the victim. There seems to be no canned response, however, for the victim creating more victims. There is a lack of moral compass. Over the last 30 years the erosion of moral direction has become obvious. The solution is simple. We must, as Jesus said, be the light of the world.

In many ways we have been busy as a church at this task. Our Boy and Girl Scout Troops have impacted generations of youth. Our Children and Youth Bible Study has been a beacon of light in the community surrounding our church. It has provided tangible spiritual and temporal blessings to its students. Several of you have been support persons to several people who have found themselves in challenging situations. With this being said, let us not get weary in well doing. This is what will prevent some of the negative headlines from ever taking place, one person at a time. We cannot wait for others to correct what takes place in our neighborhoods; we must lift the plank from our own collective eye, and the only part of our community that truly can do it is the church, empowered by God.

The Newspaper and the Bible
July 19, 1998

This past Monday Hickory Hill officially became part of Memphis. Less than a year after several residents attempted to form the city of Nonconnah, Hickory Hill joins Memphis in a quiet resolution of an eleven-year struggle. Because of this, some of these residents are ready to move to Mississippi.

In a related development, early voting began this Friday across the county. The upcoming election is projected to have the lowest turnout in years. Ironically, it is perhaps one of the most important elections in the last five years. Many of our judges are elected to the bench, and this year, the job security of several judges is on the line. Within the boundaries of the law, judges have discretion in giving sentences, and the halls of justice have become more evenhanded as they have become more multiethnic. This, in some way, is threatened by this election. We also have an opportunity to change who sits in the county sheriff's office. This change could very well take place—if we want it to.

There may be some who read this and question this subject matter in this space. I agree with Robert McAfee Brown, who in his book, *The Bible Speaks To You*, wrote, "…the minute you take your 'religion' seriously, you've got to be concerned about your fellow men, and in our kind of world concern for fellow men inevitably means concern with the political arena in which men live. Since the 'gospel' is concerned not only with individuals, but with individuals in their social relationships, it must be relevant to the way people order their social relationships in politics and government."[iii]

The issues of Hickory Hill and voter turnout are tied together as we view the future of our city and region, and we all must participate in the process of its development. This important task cannot be left to someone else—it is our collective responsibility. Many in our community recognized this importance, and they pushed in the past for our collective right to vote. Let us not neglect this hard-earned right. Please take advantage of early voting this year. It is even more important when you consider the new shift to computerized voting. Early voting will give you a chance to familiarize yourself with this new technology and avoid long lines. Voting sites are located at Mississippi Boulevard Christian Church, Greater Middle Baptist on Knight Arnold, New Salem M. B. Church on South Parkway, and in various other churches and locations across our city.

Let us all be active in this process that has a direct effect on our future. Remember, we can be like the ostrich and run from trouble by putting our head in the sand, but then we can't complain about what happens to the rest of our body.

Some Ways the Church is Needed in Our Society
November 18, 2001

Collectively we now sit one week before our formal celebration of 136 years of ministry. As we view the news, we see continued reasons why our job will never be completed. At the time this is being written, much of Afghanistan is in the control of the Northern Alliance, and the Taliban appear to be on the run or holed up in caves somewhere in inaccessible areas. On Monday, American Airlines flight 587 crashed about 5 miles from Kennedy airport on the last strip of land it would have seen between New York and Santo Domingo, Dominican Republic.

I highlight these circumstances here not to be an extension of the media, or to add my opinion to the long list of peoples' who are attempting to interpret current events. However, these events can help us see areas in which the church can be a blessing and strength in the midst of society's struggles. In this spirit, let us view some of these areas:

1. ***The church can speak out against evil.*** Those responsible for the rash of terrorism that has befallen our country should be punished. However, once they are punished the problem of evil remains. Part of the challenge of dealing with evil is to look at this question of terrorism from the perspective of the terrorists—in other words, what drives them toward this expression of evil? We must also deal with evil wherever it exists. The

church ultimately says to the world that evil can only be addressed in its fullness under the blood of Jesus. Changing individuals is the glue that begins to change unjust systems. That's what the Civil Rights Movement, anchored in the church, was all about. One of my pastoral colleagues in New York said to me this week that times like these separate the preachers from the prophets. The church and the world need to keep an ear out for the prophets of this age.

2. ***The church can create a bridge to our enemies.*** Jesus, in the Sermon on the Mount, encourages us to love our enemies, for God… *causes his sun to rise on the evil and the good, and sends rain on the righteous and the unrighteous* (Matthew 5:45). Many have brought negative critiques against the church and our nation in the past. We are not inclined, as Colin Powell often states when he refers to individuals, to suffer fools gladly. Jesus says, in Matthew 5:46, *If you love those who love you, what reward will you get? Are not even the tax collectors doing that?* We must move past our desire to God's desire for all not to perish, but come to repentance.

3. ***The church can be a place of comfort.*** Right now, the world needs comfort. The citizens of Afghanistan have lost loved ones over the course of a civil war through the rule of the Taliban, and now through our war on terrorism. War always exacts a price on the innocent and the guilty—remember, we have not yet found the guilty. The cities of New York, Washington, and Trenton, New Jersey are

undergoing trauma and grief. The loved ones who remain after the events on September 11 continue to suffer on many levels. And last but certainly not least are all the people we see and talk to in the living of our days. They may need the comfort found in the gospel. The following words remind us where our ultimate hope and anchor resides: *God [is] our refuge and strength, a very present help in trouble. Therefore will not we fear, though the earth be removed, and though the mountains be carried into the midst of the sea* (Psalm 46:1-2).

4. ***The church can be a place of hope.*** In the midst of war, uncertainty and calamity, there is no hope outside of Jesus. Let us remind ourselves of that hope, and freely share it with others in the midst of a sin-filled world; for many are looking for hope in all the wrong places. We have the one message that can be shared with others while never running out of supply for ourselves.

Our Relationship and Lifestyle
January 20, 2002

In the providence of God, January 15, 1929 was a date in which *kronos* time (the time of the clock) and *kairos* time (the right time) joined forces in Atlanta, Georgia. Doctor Martin Luther King, Jr. was a Divine vehicle who lasted on the world stage as long as a sunburst, but with a powerful impact that is still felt by many.

Doctor King's witness reminds us of the Christian's role in society. Our *relationship* with Christ should impact our *lifestyle*. The gospel, when shared, critiques every facet of human existence, based upon its influence and authority in shaping morality. A Christian in church should execute judgment based on Christian principles in the workplace, home and school. His or her posture will influence those whom he or she meets on a regular basis. This is one of the reasons Jesus referred to Christians as *the salt of the earth* (Matthew 5:13).

As we reside in 2002, we can definitively say that as a people we've come a long way. Doors that were previously sealed shut are now open. And yet, the struggle remains. African-American law enforcement workers go to a bank and are mistaken for robbers. Racial profiling, which was an issue long before 9/11, now can be hidden under the cloak of patriotism. The economic and educational achievements for many of our people are still undergoing challenges. The following words of Jesus, though directly applied to evangelism, have application in this situation: *...The harvest is plentiful but the workers are few. Ask the Lord of the harvest, therefore, to send out workers into his harvest field* (Matt.

9:37, 38). The subtle implication of this text, more clearly seen in its original language, is this: God, let me understand and be willing to go and bring in the harvest.

When we work the harvest, the community is changed for the better. This is because some outside of the church were waiting for us to live our witness and help them to change their lives all along.

How Should Christians Critique Current Events?
January 19, 2003

We remember Dr. Martin Luther King, Jr. on a day and at a time in which we reap the benefits of his vision. After morning worship, many of us will eat in places that forty years ago were off-limits or equipped with a back door "for coloreds only." This is a time in history where being "the first" African-American to hold a substantial position is not as rare as it once was. By any standard of measure, we must admit that we are blessed.

However, we should not confuse blessing with completion. In a great stroke of irony, President Bush, on what would have been the 74th birthday of Dr. King, publicly voiced his displeasure with affirmative action in university admissions, weighing in with his opinion on the case pending before the Supreme Court. In a *New York Times* article written by Neil A. Lewis dated January 16, 2003, it states that, "President Bush offered a sweeping denunciation of direct preferences for racial minorities in university admissions today and said his administration would file a brief with the Supreme Court urging that the affirmative action admissions policies at the University of Michigan be declared unconstitutional."[iv] In his address on this issue, the president said, "At their core, the Michigan policies amount to a quota system that unfairly rewards or penalizes prospective students based solely on their race." Many experts, including the former president of the University of Michigan, disagree with President Bush in how he labeled the programs.

This is a serious issue. When you combine this mindset with the potential slate of new Supreme Court justices and the erosion of some civil liberties, using the war on terrorism as a smoke screen, we run the risk of erasing some notable societal gains. With this being said, allow me to shape this critique from a Christian perspective, instead of a political view covered by Christian clothing. As you attempt to view the state of current events with the newspaper in one hand and the Bible in the other, I hope you will use the following guidelines in your deliberations:

- **Does the direction benefit the majority of people?** Dismantling affirmative action in university admissions would seriously limit diversity and opportunities for many. This decision would currently affect about 30% of the population. Its influence would also be felt by the remainder – living in circumstances less informed by diversity, thus allowing their thinking to revert to "the good old days" that weren't so great, if you remember, for us.

- **Does the direction oppress the poor?** How the poor are treated in a society is an indication of its value system. Jesus deals with this in John 12, when the issue was raised about the poor concerning some expensive ointment placed on his feet. Jesus' response in verse 8, *you will always have the poor among you,* was a commentary aimed toward the true motives of those who questioned the motives of Mary. The law, in instituting the year of jubilee, made provisions for the poor, because God is the God of all. Here are some other verses of Scripture that enlighten our view on the subject:

Proverbs 29:14: *If a king judges the poor with fairness, his throne will always be secure.*
Exodus 23:6: *Do not deny justice to your poor people in their lawsuits.*

Affirmative action in college admissions has allowed many of us to gain access to the middle class. Do we now shut the door behind us? In an article in Friday's *Washington Post* written by Mike Allen and Charles Lane, Condoleezza Rice was cited for playing a key role, "…and helped President Bush to publicly condemn race-conscious admissions policies at the University of Michigan."[v]

Will this proclamation by Bush hurt opportunities for the poor? Hmmm…

- **Does the direction oppress others?** Proverbs 29:2 raises a key point: *When the righteous thrive, the people rejoice; when the wicked rule, the people groan.* I am waiting for the preferences given to applicants that are related to graduates to be eradicated. This is affirmative action that is not addressed, but very much active. The pedigree of the privileged continues to be padded by this exception.
- **Does the direction increase greed?** Already we are beginning to see signs of a turn toward increased greed and profiteering by the "haves." I believe that it is not by accident that we have seen issues of company impropriety increase on the na-

> tional scene. On top of this, President Bush seeks an economic plan that will eliminate dividend and other taxes from the plates of the wealthiest, with the assumption that these gains will find their way to the poor. In our present climate, will this happen?

These are some of the ways I believe that Dr. King critiqued America. This is how he looked at society with the newspaper in one hand, and the Bible in the other. We must use the same lens when looking at all decisions that will affect the course of the nation and our quality of life.

CHAPTER TWO - COMMUNITY ICONS & EVERYDAY HEROES: THEY MADE A DIFFERENCE

If You Have Challenges Coping with Life, What Should You Do?
August 17, 2014

The death of Robin Williams this past week at age 63 shocked many of us. Realizing that all will eventually cross from time to eternity, none expected that his time would be now, nor thought that his departure would be self-induced – this fact increasing the collective jolt. As we soon found out, Williams' departure was tied to both depression and the impending arrival of Parkinson's disease. Many reasoned both in public and privately that if depression could help accelerate this unfortunate end for Williams, with his success and financial resources, it can do it for any of us.

The reality is that depression is real. This mental illness plays out in many different ways, depending on one's income and circumstances, but the result is often similar. Many who suffer from depression self-medicate with the liquor cabinet, or prescription and illicit drugs. Others use sex or gambling. Still others engage in reckless behavior. For example, with depression often comes low self-esteem, and when a person doesn't care much about their own well-being, they will care even less about yours. Therefore, I submit, based on anecdotal and factual evidence, that much of the senseless violence, especially among our youth, can be tied to depression. Many of us may not end our own lives like Robin Williams, but we lose our lives slowly in the midst of our despair.

In closing, let me clearly say this: If you think you may be depressed, if your emotions swing up and down, get help. If you feel hopeless, get help. If you feel powerless, get help. God provides prayer as a great empowering tool, but God has also unlocked the mysteries of the human body and mind to medicine. What you are dealing with may need the assistance of counseling to help you get and stay healthy. Many of us have insurance through our jobs that will allow us to get the help we need. Some of the quick tempers, the deep suspicions, and the dysfunctional behaviors we have can't be blamed directly on Satan, but indicate an imbalance in ourselves that can be addressed. It's that serious. The alternative is death; from either the killing fields of foolish premature departures in our midst, or the calculated yet untimely departure of those who lose hope, and make a rash decision based on cloudy, impaired vision caused by a sickness not of their making.

How to Be a Hero
May 2, 2004

Recently the various media outlets reported that Army Ranger Pat Tillman was killed in Afghanistan. He is one of the many soldiers who have given their lives across the years in service to their country. We, and in some cases the soldiers, may question the assignments, but due to duty and faithfulness to task gallant people continue to defend America. Ranger Tillman was no different. In this era those like Ranger Tillman deserve more respect because they serve in our Armed Forces through volunteerism instead of the draft.

Mr. Tillman was no different in many ways than any other person in the military. People from every town and hamlet in America have donated soldiers to the cause of our country. Ranger Tillman was first known as NFL player Pat Tillman, a safety for the Arizona Cardinals. However, this in itself was not overly unique. Many athletes over the years, including Willie Mays, Ted Williams and Joe DiMaggio, interrupted their sports career to serve in the Armed Forces. The difference lies in his choice that ran counter to our culture; he walked away from a $3.6 million contract to join the military after the attacks of September 11, 2001.

This example gives us food for thought. All of us are products of our culture in ways that are either small or great. Yet Jesus calls us to be different. He asks us not to worry in the midst of downsizing of companies, rising gas prices, nonexistent salary increases and the uncertain future. He asks us to love and pray for enemies that have abused us, lied on us, and tried to kill us mentally, emotionally or physically. In all of this Jesus asks us to follow Him in obedience, and then He will address the issues of our lives. Let us then use the example of Pat Tillman and walk against, by the leading of the Lord, the negative movements of our culture. As we think about this we may worry how we will be viewed, or whether we will be seen at all. Keep in mind however, that people don't take notice of those who go with the flow; but readily of those who, with clear, reasoned intent, go against the current of the stream. Ask some of the great people in history, like Martin Luther or Martin Luther King, Jr. Because of them, our lives have been changed for the better.

A Thought about Michael Jackson
June 28, 2009

I sit, like many of you, a day after one of the most memorable in many a year. It began with hearing about the expected demise of Farrah Fawcett. In Memphis, we then heard that arguably the best mayor in the city's history—and the first African- American one—would retire on July 10th. This was not a total surprise. Then, the big bombshell hit with a volcanic sized eruption around 5p.m. Central Time. *Michael Jackson was dead.*

We never expect things and people that are comfortable to us to leave. Our minds, for example, know that mama at some point will leave us, but when it happens, it rocks our world.

The Jackson family is our family. When you say, 'Tito" around Black folks, we aren't thinking about the former leader of Yugoslavia. "Jermaine" isn't first connected to Dupri, the rapper and producer, or O'Neal, the basketball player. And before number 23 of Chicago Bulls and Nike sneaker fame, there was only one *Michael.*

Many, especially the media, bring current focus on how he may have died, his personal troubles, and private debts. Every person possesses skeletons. Most people's skeletons aren't given any attention, to their relief and joy. The limelight, however, won't allow that comfort. While we can focus on Michael's death, bills, and family, the fact remains that these areas won't directly affect most of us. We're just nosy.

As every life preaches a sermon, I want to focus on one thing that Michael Jackson leaves us. He left talent combined with a persistent work ethic. His creative perfectionism is legendary. Coupled with hard work, this is his lasting legacy, which produced platinum albums and his status as the King of Pop.

Many of us have great talent, but lack the sufficient work ethic. Others, knowing they have limited talent, make up for this with persistence. Because of Michael Jackson's talent and hard work, the doors keeping Black artists from commercial recognition were broken down. Before Oprah, he was the megastar; and due to his efforts, Black artists now dominate, to some degree, the Billboard Top 100. Michael Jackson almost singlehandedly created the music video, and still has the bestselling album of all time.

The bottom line is simple. If Michael hadn't matched his genius with persistence, it would be scary as to what the musical and entertainment landscape would look like. God has placed similar genius in you. You may not sing, write, dance or act, but you possess something that the world won't see without you. What will the world look like if you don't share it?

What About Your Dash?
May 2, 2010

About two weeks ago Memphis and the nation said goodbye to a Civil Rights legend, Dr. Benjamin Hooks. As I sat in the funeral at the Temple of Deliverance Church of God in Christ, I pondered an interesting reality. Two long blocks east of where the funeral was being held is our very own First Baptist Church Lauderdale, the church of Dr. Hooks' youth; the soil from which he grew and from where he was ordained under the pastorate of Dr. H. Clark Nabrit in 1955. Surrounding our church is the neighborhood where Dr. Hooks was born in 1925.

Dr. Hooks was gifted to his family and the world and by God's design. He arrived on God's schedule, his last day on earth was on God's calendar, and he died just a short distance from where he was born. However, the world didn't stop and pay its respects because of the days of birth and death. It did so because of the dash in between.

Dr. Hooks made the most of the dash, which represented his life. Upon his arrival, much of the country viewed him, and people like him, as barely more than 3/5 of a person. However, upon his departure the nation mourned, flags were flown at half-staff, and the city of his birth preempted its broadcast schedule to carry his funeral. His dash was a fragrant flower that gave great benefits to many generations, and because he made the most of it, the nation and the world are better places.

We all have a dash. It is what God gave us at birth. Yes, impediments influence at times how we can use it, but it's ours. If we trust God, and live life to the fullest, we can make a difference wherever we are, but we must first take ownership of our dash.

The Difference Three People Can Make
October 9, 2011

You are now reading words typed into an iPad2, using a wireless keyboard. My iPhone 4, the best cell phone I've ever owned, is on the table in front of me. This past week, I gave the benediction for the new Unified School Board at the headquarters of Memphis City Schools, and the District Attorney of Shelby County, Amy Weirich, stopped by to introduce herself to me and to the community. Besides the goodness and power of God, all of these things took place due to a child who was adopted by working class parents, a country preacher unafraid of death, and a groundbreaking lawyer who was the first college graduate in his family.

Steve Jobs unquestionably was *the* technological innovator at this point in the digital age. He was a co-founder of Apple Inc., producer of the groundbreaking iPhone, iPod, and iPad, and a pioneer of the personal computer revolution. But he came from humble beginnings and was a college dropout.

Professor Derrick Bell was the first tenured black professor at Harvard Law School, and later the first black dean of a law school that was not historically black. He left his position at Harvard when the school wouldn't hire a minority woman professor. As the *New York Times,* on October 6, 2010 states in his obituary, "He was a pioneer of critical race theory — a body of legal scholarship that explored how racism is embedded in laws and legal institutions, even many of those intended to redress past injustices. His 1973 book, 'Race, Racism and American Law,' became a staple in law schools and is now in its sixth edition." [vi]

Reverend Fred Shuttlesworth was one of the four founding ministers of the Southern Christian Leadership Conference, enduring bombings and beatings while organizing protests in Birmingham. These protests were pivotal in laying the groundwork for much of the Civil Rights Movement afterward. He once said to a group of college students, "I tried to get killed in Birmingham and go home to God because I knew it would be better for you in Birmingham."[vii]

These three men have now framed the dash following their birthdates with one of final transition. Each one was a change agent in his own right, and their beginnings gave no warning as to the impact and influence they would wield in the world. They began life no differently than many of us, but used what they had while having a vision of a better day.

Many of us think that if we maintain what we do, things will change. The reality is that if we trust in a greater vision than we could ever imagine, while working to bring it to pass, it very likely will come true. Christians know this concept as *faith.* If we would fully practice it, what we see around us would change. Need present day evidence? You are now reading words typed into an iPad2, using a wireless keyboard. My iPhone 4...

The Death of Heavy D: It Should Make You Think...
November 13, 2011

Today many music fans across the world are shocked and saddened by the demise of Heavy D, a hip-hop icon from the '80's who passed this week at the age of 44. What endeared him to many was that he was able to be family-friendly while maintaining the edgy groove of the streets. He also never forgot the bedrock that was his Jamaican heritage, and through his music – hip-hop, R&B, and reggae – met and had fruitful conversations with his listeners.

For me, although I can't remember formally meeting him, he was like family; as he lived in the predominantly Black suburban city of Mount Vernon, just above my neighborhood in The Bronx. His family background is also similar to my own. While watching one of his videos this week that focused on Mount Vernon, it brought back memories of shopping and moving around some of those same locations.

Heavy D's death brings an interesting focus. We naturally highlight those in the public eye, and any adverse circumstances surprise us as if one's celebrity status is an impenetrable force field. These types of shocking deaths remind us of the frailty of life. The truth is that we plan--or do nothing--as if we will be here forever. The reality is that everyone is walking toward the grave, for we all will eventually become acquainted with death's sting.

What we should remember most as we say goodbye to Heavy D is that he made the most of his life and personhood. As a musician, he sang and wrote songs; most notably the theme to the "In Living Color" TV show. He was also an actor. His persona was so bright and well-loved that when he made his final TV appearance about two weeks ago, the studio audience was on their feet. Considering this example, look in the mirror right now. Have you made the most of your life? When people see you coming, are they excited or disappointed? Do you encourage the best out of others? All of us come into this world to contribute to the vast opus of humanity, regardless of our circumstances, and if you and I abdicate our responsibility in this regard, we live beneath our privilege.

The final question is obvious: Are you and I prepared, at a moment's notice, to let go of this world for eternity? We assume that we have the luxury of extended time, but we don't control *chronos* time (the time of the clock), nor the end of our personal time. At one point I assumed, without giving it much thought, that Luther Vandross, Michael Jackson, Heavy D, and an assortment of friends and family would always be around. Yet my conversations about them today reside in the land of the past tense. After we make the most of our time, there waits the reality of life eternal, where we must prepare in advance for Divine fellowship. God awaits us, because we responded to the Eternal overture while in the land of the living.

I can hear the words of Jesus, *Here I am! I stand at the door and knock. If anyone hears my voice and opens the door, I will come in and eat with him, and he with me* (Revelation 3:20).

Why Your Neighbor Should be a Samaritan
May 12, 2013

Luke 10:29-33, 36-37: *But he wanted to justify himself, so he asked Jesus, "And who is my 41neighbour?" In reply Jesus said: "A man was going down from Jerusalem to Jericho, when he fell into the hands of robbers. They stripped him of his clothes, beat him and went away, leaving him half dead. A priest happened to be going down the same road, and when he saw the man, he passed by on the other side. So too, a Levite, when he came to the place and saw him, passed by on the other side. But a Samaritan, as he 41traveled, came where the man was; and when he saw him, he took pity on him..."Which of these three do you think was a 41neighbour to the man who fell into the hands of robbers?" The expert in the law replied, "The one who had mercy on him." Jesus told him, "Go and do likewise."*

There was a busy Cleveland street, where children played and the mail came every weekday. Neighbors looked out for each other and fellowshipped through barbecues and other social gatherings. Yet there were at least three young girls who lived in the shadows. Like the man who was robbed in the above text, they found themselves off a popular thoroughfare and in need of help.

Their church didn't check on them. The school got tired of sending notices home. The amber alert got drowned out by newly minted ones, especially those from neighborhoods more tony and prosperous. The businessmen with means didn't stop in that neighborhood but passed quickly through on their way to other places. But a dishwasher named Charles Ramsey, with an un-cashed paycheck in his pocket, heard the cry coming from the shadows and answered the call. Today, three women who had been missing for ten years or more, and a young child, now enjoy the routine freedoms afforded to all of us because of his actions.

The problem, however, is that Charles Ramsey is a Samaritan. His "look" isn't right, and his syntax is worse. *What happened to a suit for a national interview, instead of the backwards baseball cap? Why won't you take the award money? Don't you wash dishes for a living? And we now find out that you have a criminal record and you've done jail time.* We don't like Samaritans—you know, those people who aren't like "us."

In the above scripture, the expert in the law asked Jesus the question, "Who is my neighbor?" Jesus then tells the parable of a common, well-travelled road that was known to have bandits, and how the people who were expected to show mercy didn't come through for the injured victim of a robbery. The despised one—the Samaritan, the half breed with strange ways—took action and demonstrated the mechanics of being a neighbor.

Jesus' point, which should be ours, is maybe we shouldn't get caught up in the exterior packaging of a person, but instead place our focus on what comes from within. Then all of us will start looking more like Samaritans.

How Would You Answer His Question?
December 15, 2013

Over the past week, the world saluted a great icon as it said goodbye. As it remembered Nelson Rolihlahla Mandela, various versions of who people thought he was were presented to us. Some saw him as a freedom fighter for his people, the indigenous Africans in the nation of South Africa. Others saw him as a conciliatory grandfather whose smile disarmed opponents. Still others painted him as the face of forgiveness, because after enduring 27 years of prison—18 of which were in notorious Robben Island—he emerged as one seemingly without bitterness. Another perspective showed him as a bold revolutionary who was uncompromising in his beliefs for a democratic South Africa. The truth is that like a multi-layered cake, you can find all of these things in the one man, depending on the circumstances and prism through which you view his life.

How then, should we understand and see the wider impact of a Nelson Mandela? Perhaps the answer can be found in the African concept of *ubuntu*. Archbishop Desmond Tutu explains this concept best in his book, *No Future Without Forgiveness*, saying, "A person with ubuntu is open and available to others, affirming of others, does not feel threatened that others are able and good, based from a proper self-assurance that comes from knowing that he or she belongs in a greater whole and is diminished when others are humiliated or diminished, when others are tortured or oppressed."[viii] Mandela's life was the embodiment of ubuntu. In other words, ubuntu causes you to fight for your people, changing tactics when you deem it necessary, but never deviating from your goal. Ubuntu causes you to say while waiting for a judge's decision, "During my lifetime I have dedicated myself to this struggle of the African people. I have fought against white domination, and I have fought against black domination. I have cherished the ideal of a democratic and free society in which all people live together in harmony and with equal opportunities. It is an ideal which I hope to live for and to achieve. But if needs be, it is an ideal for which I am prepared to die."[ix] This same understanding causes you to shape a Truth and Reconciliation Commission when you become President of your country, in order to assist its healing. Ubuntu takes the principles that you learned as a part of your Christian faith and expands upon them for the good of all.

This leads to our next question: Can we emulate the life and witness of Nelson Mandela? If you begin to really understand the concept of ubuntu, the answer is unequivocally yes. The point of Mandela's witness was collective consciousness, which drove his every decision. From passing up earlier prison releases with conditions, to his perseverance along the journey to where his final remains will be laid to rest, his focus stayed in ubuntu. In a video discussing this subject, Mr. Mandela said, "Ubuntu does not mean that people should not enrich themselves. *The question therefore is: Are you going to do so in order to enable the community around you to be able to improve?*"[x]

As we celebrate and mourn his passing, and as we discuss his legacy, the more important issue is, how would you answer his question?

The Improbable Often Becomes Possible
February 8, 2015

A week ago Saturday, Serena Williams, arguably the best women's tennis player ever, won her 19th Grand Slam title with her finals victory at the Australian Open. Even the most casual tennis observer knows that Serena's fast, explosive serve and returns overwhelm many of her opponents. Many times we watch her matches with expectations of her victory, and merely sit in awe of her artistry. What makes this last victory remarkable is that Serena has the number one ranking and another Grand Slam title at an age when many previous tennis greats faded in their skill sets or retired. The only one who appears to be in the way of Serena's continued playing career and its success is Serena alone.

The most intriguing aspect of this scenario is that we either forget or take for granted its improbable beginnings. In our imagination, let's transport ourselves back to Compton, California in the mid 1980's. A father, coming from a hardscrabble life in Shreveport, Louisiana, wanted his two youngest daughters to become millionaires by playing an improbable sport—tennis. Richard Williams took his admiration of tennis that he watched on TV to reading instruction manuals, and brought his daughters to Compton's municipal courts, made of concrete and strewn with glass. Many asked, "Who is this crazy Black man with these crazy braided Black girls?" for they went against the grain of what tennis players looked like and where tennis players came from, even when measured against Black tennis players of that day.

Richard Williams understood that an audacious goal has nothing to do with what others think about you but has everything to do with your attitude and execution. And now, 30 years later, his genius is obvious. As we celebrate Black History Month, we should see that this genius isn't unique to the Williams family, but resides in each of us. Through faith in God, our ancestors maneuvered the scraps and lack before them, and made the impossible possible. Today, we often take the possible and render it impossible. In doing this, we in essence tell the "cloud of witnesses" in Hebrews 12 watching us that their heavy lifting was in vain; for the lighter loads we bear, in our opinion, are too formidable for us.

God works through and uses our impossibilities and improbabilities as a billboard, displaying both His power and our tenacity when our trust centers in the Lord. It's time for the world to see God through our work.

Be Who You Is
June 12, 2016

By the time you read this, the sports icon who was larger than life, who could "float like a butterfly and sting like a bee," will receive his Muslim rites and be laid to rest in a ceremony for the general public. There has never been, and will not be again, a public personality like Muhammad Ali. He coupled phenomenal, one of a kind boxing skills with a unique combination of showmanship and marketing acumen never before seen in his sport. Along with this was an attribute that all of us would do well to emulate – conviction. Ali understood the intersection of his spiritual life and its secular application. It influenced his business decisions and led him to reject being drafted into the armed services, regardless of the consequences. It also caused those who may have initially disagreed with him to ultimately respect and support his decision to resist.

Having an understanding of how our spiritual life affects our decisions makes all the difference in the world. For many, their spiritual life remains segregated to the confines of Sunday morning. However, if we claim to have a *relationship* with Jesus Christ, we then remember that we are the light of the world. We are to illuminate and affect what is around us, not the reverse. We saw how this should work while watching the life of Ali, who lived this principle in the midst of his Muslim reality.

We must also remember the takeaway of conviction. Conviction caused Ali to miss the prime of his boxing life, and he almost went to jail. Yet he never wavered. He also never denied the richness of who he was as a Black man. What does this mean? An old sermon illustration fits here. The story is told of a group of Soviet soldiers who disrupted a church worship service in staunch communist Russia. "All of you in this service who are willing to die for this Jesus, line up against this wall." Men and women ran out of the church, yet a few remained and did what the soldiers asked. The soldiers then put down their rifles, saying, "Good...now we can worship with you now that the pretenders are gone."

The bottom line?

"Be who you is, cuz if you be what you ain't, then you ain't what you is."[xi]

CHAPTER THREE - GOD AND THE HOLIDAYS

What is Independence?
July 7, 1996

This page is often composed during the period that stretches from Thursday to Friday morning. During that time, I ponder all of the things that have happened during the course of the week. Often the topic of the week is obvious; sometimes it isn't. This week, as I was having a casual conversation with some of our members, the hour was growing late, and I mentioned that I had to go home and begin working on this page. Their reply was, "Say something about Independence Day; *our* independence."

On the surface, as I sat there, this idea sounded slightly corny. How many times have I heard people use misguided symbolism during this holiday, in a vain attempt to motivate people? However, as I continued to think about this request, it made more and more sense. I also began to reflect on the tone of our conversation. We were talking about the book, *At the River I Stand*, an account of the 1968 sanitation strike. I also met one of the Tuskegee airmen, who had graduated from Penn State in the 1940's with ten other African-Americans. This reminded me of my own graduation from Brandeis University in 1982 with six other African-Americans. When I reflect on the need for the sanitation strike, on these numbers and the time span in which they happened, one thought, among many, became much clearer. The more things change, the more they stay the same.

What should independence mean to us? African-Americans are presently enjoying, on a collective level, the highest standard of living in our history. Yet, this is also one of our most self-destructive periods. We have more choices of living accommodations and jobs, yet redlining and racism are alive and well. And all the while, sin is rampant in the land. In many ways, we have taken our eyes off of the goal, thinking that the assimilation of choice—where we eat, drink, and spend—is the ultimate destination instead of actually being deserved equality, while forsaking our own economic viability.

True independence is a return to the bridges that brought us over—Jesus, hard, honest work, and a commitment to each other. Living in relationship to Christ frees you from the material rat race and the focus on self-destruction. It also places within you the desire to seek the salvation and security of others. My brothers and sisters, this is what evangelism is all about. As we begin to be change agents in our community, we will bring back to mind the true meaning of the word independence.

Happy Birthday America: What Does This Mean for Us? A Christoafrocentric Vision July 6, 1997

This past Friday was the 221st birthday of the United States of America; a noble experiment in which the rights and freedoms of the individual, at least in theory, are held in the highest regard. In light of this, I began to reflect on the meaning of freedom for me, and those who look like me.

We, the descendants of great African kingdoms and slaves, have the highest standard of living across the African diaspora. Whether we go to Brazil, which has the largest number of African descendants outside of Africa, or to Africa itself, we see how we in America have been blessed in this way. In addition, in spite of the reference to "3/5ths of a man," the Constitution and its amendments allow for broad freedoms. The issue has always been how America has acted out the social and economic realities created by these legalities. Jim Crow and affirmative action are two ways in which these realities have shaped the legal system.

What does this mean? The history of our country seems to work in 100-year cycles. Presently for African-Americans, we live in "the best of times and the worst of times." We prosper materially and die morally and spiritually. It appears that the window of opportunity is beginning to swing in the opposite direction. 1896 and *Plessy* vs. *Ferguson* looks poised and ready to make a reappearance. This time, however, we will have no excuse for being unprepared.

In saying these things, we recognize that ultimate freedom cannot come from a government, but from the Lord. As finite humans, we must work through the confines of nationhood, but our permanent citizenship belongs to a land in the heavens. Therefore, we must be, as one church motto says, "unashamedly African- American and unapologetically Christian." In other words, we reach people through the reality of their culture, and expose them to the good news. Taking this stance—being "Christoafrocentric"—is the only way we will reach many of our brothers and sisters. This is not a cosmetic reality only taught through kente cloth, but an interior work weaving first through the Bible and reshaping culture. In doing this, we will lead many from the darkness of their slavery into the marvelous light of ultimate freedom.

The Last Push into a New Year
December 30, 2001

Today we greet the last Sunday of an eventful year. On the first Sunday in January, it may have appeared to some that we would never get here, for the landscape of the year seemed long and tedious. Yet in the blink of an eye we sit at the dawn of 2002.

This past year our lives, our church and our nation have been through challenges. Many of us have had unique situations transpire in our lives and those of our loved ones. At the time of the storm, it may have seemed that you and yours would sink under the load. Churches always go through the ebb and flow of a job description diametrically in opposition to the world. And our country has been changed forever since the events of 9/11.

Challenges will always intersect with life's journey. However, God has created one method among many to help us through life's maze of troubles. This ingenious method is time. God uses time to help change circumstances, allow us to see solutions and to experience His presence during challenged times. The times of our greatest spiritual growth happen in the fields of sorrow and adversity. We then learn how good God is.

God also uses time to bring healing and create new landscapes of opportunity. In less than two days, 2002 will be God's vehicle to bring this to pass. All of us will be able to shed the old year and use this new canvas. It is my prayer that we will use the new year in the service of God to increase our love, fellowship and commitment to Christ and each other.

How Should We Share Christmas Every Day?
December 15, 2002

Today we observe the Christmas season with the 62nd Annual rendition of George Frederic Handel's *Messiah*. It is the oldest observance of this work in any African-American church in Memphis and was birthed during the full strength of Jim Crow. Viewing this causes us to look with great focus on the climate during the first Christmas season and our present one. In the time of Jesus' birth, the Roman Empire was making its way toward its eventual decline, concluding with the fall of Rome in 410 AD. Leadership was self-serving, and guilty of the worst behavior. Octavian, the emperor during Jesus' birth, became known and is referred to in Scripture as Augustus (*reverend* in Latin). The emperor Nero killed his stepbrother, mother and wife, and later blamed Christians for the fire that consumed half of Rome. This marked the beginning of the first Roman persecution.

We presently find a world potentially poised at the brink of war. We also find a country where using the distraction of the "war on terror" as a smoke screen is the order of the day while the economy, civil rights, and quality of life issues are being adversely challenged. During this term the Supreme Court is scheduled to hear the case *Virginia* vs. *Black, et al.*, where at issue is a state statute that bans cross burning as a action "with the intent to intimidate." The question being raised is whether this statute is a violation of free speech. The case before the Supreme Court involves two incidents of cross burnings, consolidated for the court, that occurred within months of each other in 1998. The first incident involved three teenagers who tried to burn a cross on a neighbor's lawn; the second was an organized Ku Klux Klan rally on private property where a large cross was burned. Nearby homeowners and motorists were able to see the burning. The ACLU hired an African-American lawyer to defend the rally's organizer, saying his right to free speech was violated, however disturbing the speech. Another case that is pending is an affirmative action suit involving the University of Michigan's law school. In an article in the *Detroit Free Press* on May 16, 2002 entitled, "Affirmative Action Case Expected to Reach High Court," Lino Graglia, a prominent University of Texas Law School professor, states, "Americans should have no illusions about how the case ultimately will be decided. The law and the constitution will have nothing do with the decision. It will all be about individual judgments." Referring to judges' political and philosophical biases that he said inevitably come into play in such high-stakes decisions, he added, "We want to pretend that these things are decided on the basis of the law, but that's perfect fiction."[xii]

These cases are important for us to view because the church was the incubator that created much positive change during the last 40 to 50 years. This happened because people, such as Dr. King, understood that "injustice anywhere is a threat to justice everywhere." They also understood that they were their "brother's keeper." Although the forces against their movement were great, I believe this particular witness of Scripture gave them strength, *Greater is He that is in you, than he that is in the world* (1 John 4:4). They also knew that the direction of history needed adjustment. For them, the quote attributed to the philosopher George Santayana rang true: "Those who cannot remember the past are condemned to repeat it."

The events of the past two years are gaining momentum, causing us to re-examine who we are, where we are and what we believe. We must re-anchor our trust in the One who intersected with humanity during this season over 2,000 years ago to give hope and reconnection to God. Then we, through our personal and collective witness, can point men and women to a relationship with Jesus Christ, and encourage responsible, caring actions toward each other as embodied in these words: *"Love the Lord your God with all your heart and with all your soul and with all your mind'" This is the first and greatest commandment. And the second is like it: "Love your neighbor as yourself." All the Law and the Prophets hang on these two commandments* (Matt. 22:37-40).

A Kind Word on Father's Day
June 17, 2012

Today is Father's Day, a time set aside to commemorate the importance of fathers in our society. Often, we make fun of this day, and some even question its validity in light of statistics suggesting that most births in this part of the 21st century take place outside of marital unions. Therefore, many ask, "Why honor someone who in many cases isn't present?"

Trouble is, we may have created this scenario by thought, word and deed. The concept of a Father's Day began at the turn of the last century. Unlike Mother's Day, which was met with enthusiasm, Father's Day was met with laughter. This was during the time when fathers were in the home across all ethnicities in America. However, two-parent homes coupled with policies crafted around public assistance, which created benefits for households without a man in the home, was the beginning of a recipe for family disintegration.

In the Word, marriage between husband and wife is a symbol of one's relationship to God, and children are a blessing from the Lord. Isn't it interesting that as our society grows more Godless, our homes are now much more fragmented? Recognizing what God intended for us should cause us to give honor to both Mother and Father.

On this day, look past the imperfections, real or imagined, of your father. Look past what may be family fragmentation due to reasons that have nothing to do with you, and realize that all of us have flaws. In Matthew 7:15, Jesus gives the example of looking past the beam in our own eye to the speck in someone else's. The issues we may have with our father is the beam in our eye we should address. This will enable us to better see and render grace to our father, even if undeserved. Thank God for your father, and if you are able, let him know you love him. Perhaps with these simple acts we can begin to put back together the blessing of family and societal structure that God intended.

CHAPTER FOUR - CROSS POLLINATION: CONVERSATIONS BETWEEN VARIOUS PLATFORMS

STATEMENT FROM THE TENNESSEE PROGRESSIVE BAPTIST COUNCIL[xiii]
SUNDAY, AUGUST 14, 2016

We the undersigned represent the churches of Tennessee Progressive Baptist Council, a state group aligned with the Progressive National Baptist Convention (PNBC). The PNBC was the denominational home of Dr. Martin Luther King, Jr., and many of its churches and pastors were on front lines with him marching for justice and equality. As a denomination and a council, PNBC has always addressed these issues.

This history causes the Tennessee Progressive Baptist Council (TPBC) to respond to the recent turmoil in our nation. The deaths of Alton Sterling, Philandro Castile, and the shooting of Charles Kinsey are the recent editions in a trend that goes back decades. Here in Memphis, the death of Darrius Stewart, along with the fatal shootings of 24 persons by the Memphis Police Department in five years with no indictments, raises questions of the unjust application of appropriate force when law enforcement encounters people of color. In the midst of this, the voice of the church, except for rare occasions, has been noticeably silent. In light of this, we the TPBC have decided to speak.

We, the Tennessee Progressive Baptist Council:

- Demand the end of African Americans being tried by the gun of a rogue police officer than by a jury of twelve in a court of law.

- Say plainly that the murder of unarmed citizens is never acceptable.
- We also demand fair and equal treatment from the judicial system when involving cases of people of color.

In addition:

- We pledge to work with local, state, and federal legislators to shape the policy which has allowed the culture of unjust treatment to exist.
- We will also continue to work, as we have been, in addressing the violence in our communities, which is a separate issue.

As we state our position, we also wish to clarify that we affirm the worth and work of law enforcement. In fact, in our churches are police officers, some of whom, past and present, have been of high rank in the police force. Recently, misguided individuals have taken on the task of killing police officers. The unjust killing and shooting of African Americans and the assassination of innocent police officers is unacceptable.

In our community some have seemingly rushed to support the police while ignoring the issue that was first present, which is the unarmed, unjust killing of people of color by law enforcement. However, we feel that if we address the worth of Black lives, all other issues with fall into place.

In closing, we call on clergy, the faith community, and others of good will across ethnicities to stand with us in affirming the value of Black lives and the issue of blatant, selective police brutality. In doing so we affirm the worth of all humanity.[xiv]

CHURCHES

Beulah Baptist Church
Rev. Anthony D. Henderson, Pastor

First Baptist Church, Lauderdale
Dr. Noel G. L. Hutchinson, Jr., Pastor
President, Tennessee Progressive Baptist Council

Gifts of Life Ministries
Dr. Andre Johnson, Pastor

Greater Mount Zion Baptist Church
Rev. Wendell Coward, Pastor

Greater Middle Baptist Church
Rev. William McKinley Jackson, Pastor

Greater White Stone Baptist Church,
Rev. Roger R. Brown, Pastor

Metropolitan Baptist Church,
Dr. Reginald L. Porter, Pastor

Monumental Baptist Church
Rev. Wade Bryant, Pastor

Morning View Baptist Church,
Rev. Alvin Fleming, Pastor

Mt. Moriah Baptist Church, Carnes
Dr. Harvey Jackson, Pastor

Mount Vernon Baptist Church, Westwood
Dr. James L. Netters, Pastor
Rev. Melvin Watkins, Co-Pastor

Salem Gilfield Baptist Church
Rev. Stanford Hunt, Pastor
Second Vice President, Tennessee Progressive Baptist Council

Saint John Baptist Church, Pendelton
Dr. James L, Delaney, Pastor
First Vice President, Tennessee Progressive Baptist Council

Serenity Baptist Church
Rev. Guilermo Benitez, Pastor

Facebook—Why?
August 1, 2017

I'm at the Neighborhood Night Out downtown at Central Station. When I got out of the car I encountered the tactical unit owned by the Memphis Police Department.

Now the neighborhood associations do the planning for this night. Who thought it was a good idea to have a killing machine present? This is the same type of vehicle used against our people during apartheid. It also appears when we "riot." Tell me in our history when this has been used against someone other than people of color? What message should I take away from this? Or is this a case of "since it doesn't affect you, it's not a thought for you?" Either way...I really can't say all of what I'm thinking...smh

Facebook—Somebody Saw It—Be Careful What You Post on Facebook
August 2, 2017

Beloveds, be careful of what you post on Facebook. You really don't know WHO'S WATCHING!!! My post from last night about the Neighborhood Night Out was seen, and, long story short, a segment, God willing, will air on channel 24 tonight (Wednesday) at 10:00 p.m.!

Trust, it's not about being on TV (I'm on often enough). I hope the message is sound. But beyond that, the lesson for today is BE CAREFUL WHAT YOU POST ON FB.

SOMEBODY'S WATCHIIIIIINNNNNNG YOOOOOOOOUUUUUUUUU....[xv]

Pay Attention: The Obvious Isn't Always So
August 6, 2017

The obvious isn't always so.

It often requires thought and vigilance. It requires some knowledge of the context and circumstances. I learned this over the past week. As told to us by the website:

[N]ational [-N]ight [O]ut is an annual community-building campaign that promotes police-community partnerships and neighborhood camaraderie to make our neighborhoods safer, more caring places to live. National Night Out enhances the relationship between neighbors and law enforcement while bringing back a true sense of community. Furthermore, it provides a great opportunity to bring police and neighbors together under positive circumstances[xvi].

As you may have heard, I went to a local National Night Out event at Central Station. Knowing in advance its purpose, I was appalled to see a tactical unit from the Memphis Police Department present. Since 9/11, the Department of Defense, through its 1033 program, makes surplus military equipment available to local government. Without thinking too hard about it, military equipment is used during war to kill people. Do we need this equipment for quality law enforcement in our country? Are we in partnership with the police department to encourage the militarization of our police? All of these questions hit me as Rebecca and I pulled up to Central Station and saw the tactical unit.

I also had a flashback.

Last November, I went to the Apartheid Museum in Johannesburg, and saw up close the South African version of our unit. The best way to describe it is to say it is a killing machine. It can roll over cars and some trucks with ease. It has slots on two sides for machine guns, and it is bullet and explosion proof. One of these trucks can do great damage to a neighborhood; two or three would destroy it. When I stepped out of the truck, *after* seeing pictures and video of how these trucks killed many a Black South African, I had to pray through my rage, asking God, after I gathered myself, to use my rage constructively. I learned from a reliable source that the newer tactical unit we have is like the South African one. The one I saw was the older, smaller one—the "baby" killing machine, I guess.

Think about when you've seen these trucks in action. Think about who they've been used against. Think about rolling them out for display in a city that is almost 70% Black. Think about the fact that they were almost used around the I-40 bridge a year ago. Oh, and by the way, we had some of our members on that bridge during that protest. These tactical units aren't designed to work in partnership with the community. When they are rolled out it means that something is definitely wrong and imbalanced. In my conversation on site with the person from the department that made this possible, I wasn't sure that they were even bothered by the perverse symbolism this unit brought to a night when they were supposed to be in partnership with the community.

The obvious isn't always so. We must continue to watch and pray. God is in control.

What a Movement Can Do[xvii]
December 24, 2017

Wednesday night was a great one in the annals of Memphis history. That which was created as a tool of psychological bondage was removed from its perch of prominence. The statue of Nathan Bedford Forrest, erected not as an historical marker, but a guidepost of the Jim Crow laws made official by the Supreme Court just a few years before, came down. The statue of Jefferson Davis, erected during the height of the Civil Rights Movement as a show of disrespect to Black folk, also came down.

Last night showed the power of a movement, which started with Walter and D'Army Bailey, Lasimba Gray, T. O'Neal Crivens, and many others. It was fought by others who happened to be in high places. Keith Norman and Beverly Roberston come to mind. Clergy also came together. I remember during a press conference at the Forrest statue how Rev. Maurice Dickerson expressed his deep feelings as a native Memphian and a veteran. Your pastor, as some of you know, was involved. There are countless others whose names are known only by God who were a part of this movement that culminated last night.

The tip of this long spear was Tami Sawyer and takeemdown901. If not for their activism and constant, consistent belligerence over the last year, taking up the gauntlet from those I mentioned who went before, the statues would still have their previous homes. Ultimately, Mayor Strickland, hearing the overwhelming voice of the people, crafted a plan that was executed with precision; and

Deacon Van Turner (the *deacon* before his name is not a typo) helped this effort in a powerful way.

Some, even whom are Black, don't get it. They say, "What about ____________ (fill in the blank with your 'favorite' or 'pet peeve' issue)." Last time I checked, we can walk and chew gum at the same time. The psychological symbols had to go, especially on the eve of the 50th anniversary of the assassination of Dr. King. To me, the removal of the statues was a much-needed dose of preventative medicine. The futures of many a person was saved, and the souls of many wounded have been healed through this action.

As we celebrate the arrival of the Christ child tomorrow, remember that He also came as a change agent. He came to both restore our relationship with God, and set Israel on the right course. This couldn't happen without change.

Wednesday night was a victory for a new Memphis. This should be a template for what we can do to make our city great. Let us now take aim at some of the other issues in our city, attacking them with the same intensity, and watch those giants fall...or be removed.

Facebook—Someone is Paying Attention
December 21, 2017

This, I hope, is my final post today. Contrary to what some of you may think, I don't major in Facebook, lol! Please read to the end.

I've read some posts today where several felt there wasn't appropriate thanks given to the activists who pressed the issue for the Confederate statues to come down. Guess what? There wasn't. Others showed the eventual solution of privatizing the parks in order to take the statues down long before the process started in October. Guess what? That's true. I remember reading the original post. Some are upset that the mayor didn't call takeemdown901 by name in his remarks. Well, I could have told you that wasn't happening.

If you fall into one of these camps, ask yourself this question, "Do I do what I do for the applause, or because of the greater good?" People will dog you, and your own will scandalize your name. You will be known as God's ambassador today and the spawn of Satan tomorrow. Even with all of that, most times the applause won't come. Ask Dr. King about his life AFTER his speech at Riverside Church. Better yet, ask Jesus about how they did Him.

Yet, I know how you feel. I've been right there. Activism is thankless work which will never be fully appreciated until after you're gone. So let me say this: I APPRECIATE YOU! Every denial, every thought, every sacrifice on behalf of US has not been lost on me. Also know this, SOMEONE is paying attention who can parse through every intention and every effort, and when your assignment is done, waits to greet you with a party just for you – starting with these important words:

WELL DONE.

I'm not Him, but let me say to you right now, well done.

Facebook—Read a Book
January 16, 2018

On this snowy day in Memphis, let me suggest something that some of our parents used to tell us back in the day...

Read a book.

There was a time when a parent would sacrifice and pay for a set of encyclopedias in installments. My mother bought two sets like that for me. Others, who didn't or couldn't make that sacrifice, TOOK their children to the library; getting them a library card while acquainting them with its inner workings.

Read a book.

Why am I saying this? Well, over the past few days, there have been social media debates over what President Trump said, or allegedly said, about Haiti and African nations. He called them "shithole" countries. No, I didn't blur out the profanity because you need to see it, and understand that it came from your president. YOUR president. No, I didn't vote for him either, but he is OUR president.

Read a book.

Many of you, friends in real life, are living epistles to the power of education. It appalls me then when I hear otherwise smart people, and the sheeple that follow them, rely on simple news bytes to be informed on complex issues. Today, I've seen people dwell on the poverty of

Haiti and some parts of Africa as justification, to some degree, of what the president said. Others have made it an "us vs. them," and "so he wasn't talking about me" issue. Still others politicized it, saying that Clinton was guilty of far worse in sending Haitians back from our shores some years ago, and using this to say that we are giving more weight to words vs. deeds.

Read a book.

Here is what's missing. Everyone talks about the fact that Haiti is poor. Very few ask why, because they assume they know. The same could be said about Africa, which isn't a country but a CONTINENT made up of 54 countries created out of colonization by powers unconcerned with existing nations and ethnic groups.

Read a book. Please.

Haiti is the Haiti we see now in part because after it became the world's first Black republic, it was ostracized by the world, especially the US, because other countries were afraid that the power of insurrection would destabilize their own situations. Haiti was the richest colony of France, and because it was now free, France had to have a garage sale and unload a sizable chunk of North America to a fledgling country. This sale doubled the size of this new country that had only been independent itself for less than 50 years. We know this transaction as the Louisiana Purchase. Some who are reading this live in that territory right now. Thank Haiti for your home, but also realize it came at a cost to them. France demanded, and got, reparations from Haiti that were paid well into the 20th century. Under Woodrow

Wilson, the most racist president until our current one, we occupied Haiti while also controlling its treasury. As long as this post is now, time doesn't permit me to get into how we, the U.S., have been meddling in the affairs of many nations in the Western Hemisphere, and our connections to the World Bank – which is equivalent to the payday loan institutions in every 'hood. Realize that the colonial powers in Africa also did their version of subjugation.

Read a book.

Everything I cited comes from reading. I could lightly dig and cite references, but you can do that yourself. I've given you a starting place.

Read. Please.

What's my point? Take in what you see even as you hear critique. Then you will be better able to understand what you see. If these truly are "shithole" countries, the powers that be shaped the hole, made most of the feces, and now turn around and call them names. That is actually the biggest insult of all.

Facebook—About Wolfchase Mall— The Power of "All of Y'all"[xviii] December 27, 2017

Several people have tagged me in their posts concerning what happened at the Wolfchase Mall. For those outside of Memphis, young people sent texts and inboxes all day through social media to gather at the mall. Once they got there, fights broke out, and three people were shot. Thank God no one was seriously injured. One video shows a young man running out of the mall, dropping a gun, and then picking it up.

Today, every armchair philosopher has an opinion as to what's wrong with our young people. Many of them, who haven't cracked an egg's worth of real life solutions, have all the answers. The most genius of the bunch will find a way to tie in the statue removal as part of the problem. To all of you zealots and others of that ilk, here is the perfect phrase for you: sit your butt down! Thank you.

I had a conversation with a friend in October who was visiting Memphis. He lives about five blocks from where we grew up – by choice. He told me about a conversation he had with his teenage son about the neighborhood, and how in awe the son was as to what the neighborhood used to be. They also talked about how much the neighborhood had changed for the worse. What does that mean? Less camaraderie. Less connectedness. Less caring. Less communal activity. In the summertime, kids were outside in great numbers, playing street games on every block. Now, you can drive up and down those same streets and see houses but no children.

What has changed? What's my point? Is it the youth? Well, there were "bad seeds" back then, and their issues weren't necessarily determined by their household income. Wolf-chase is in one of the more affluent areas of the city. Yes, you have pockets of poverty nearby, but the mall is in what is considered a safe neighborhood.

Consider the following thoughts, and put them together for a comprehensive fit:
1) To have a decent economic lifestyle, many mothers work more than one job. For one parent households, that takes away supervision. This is the case with many a student.

2) Economic frustration. Do I really need to explain this one?

3) Lack of appropriate role models and resolution skills. Many of our adults don't have these, so how do you expect our youth to have them?

4) THE COMMUNITY HAS CHANGED. In the past, the community helped the children of weak parents. The community directed those children long before they got to this point, and the community didn't wait for elected officials to jump in. The community handled its business! Here is the last piece of the equation. I grew up in a two-family house one block from the projects. What does that mean? All types of our folk, with all types of incomes and backgrounds lived on my block and around me. Some of them will read this post and confirm what I'm saying. We learned to live together and rely on each other. I didn't even know the meaning of "bougie" black folk until I left

for college! I grew up and dealt with the talented tenth and hood rats at the same time, and I still roll like that now. Maybe that's the real problem--we look down on one another and forget that Pookie and Ray Ray are KINFOLK.

A somewhat well-known blogger in our national community indicates a difference between native born and immigrant Blacks, saying that the immigrants ought to check "white" on the census form (a paraphrase). I've heard others talk about those who have less as if they are a scourge, the contagion of our people. The issue is if we don't get together, we won't solve this or any other problem.

There are organizations working in every city to combat these issues. We don't need more organizations, we need more workers. Find where you can roll up your sleeves and help. Start with your family, your block, your neighborhood.

LET'S GET TO WORK.THERE'S PLENTY OF IT.

Wolfchase Galleria Shooting – A Dire Message from Unsupervised Youth[xix]

Noel G.L. Hutchinson, Guest columnist
(The *Commercial Appeal*)
Published online 12:00 p.m. CT January 1, 2018; also in the January 2 printed edition

For a week we've heard and talked about what happened the day after Christmas at Wolfchase Galleria.

On that day, young people sent messages all day through social media to meet there. Once they arrived, fights broke out and three people were shot. Thank God, no one was seriously injured. Seven people were arrested. This was one of several similar incidents that happened in malls across the country over the past two years, targeting the day after Christmas.

Because of this incident and others, every armchair philosopher has an opinion about what's wrong with our young people. Some genius will find a way to cast the Confederate statue removals and other related issues as part of the problem. This is conflation -- blending separate issues together and making them seem like the same one. Doing this is really a cover for continuing the confusion that keeps many people inactive and frustrated. It produces nothing but hot air. Well, it may help to keep us warm in a cold winter.

How do we address the mall incident as a symptom of deeper problems? I offer one perspective that comes from a conversation I had with a friend this past October who came to Memphis on business.

My friend lives, by choice, about five blocks from where we both grew up. He told me about a conversation he had with his teenage son about our old neighborhood, and how in awe his son was as he learned what the neighborhood used to be. They also talked about how much the neighborhood had changed for the worse. There is less camaraderie, less caring, and less communal activity.

In our day, in the summertime, kids were outside in great numbers, playing street games on every block. Nowadays you can drive up and down those same streets and see houses but no children. What changed? Is it the youth? Well, there were “bad seeds” back then and their issues weren't necessarily determined by their household income.

Consider this: to have a decent economic lifestyle, many single parents work more than one job. This leads to a lack of supervision for many youth. Add to that poor role models and poorly modeled conflict resolution skills. How do we expect youth to have skills they aren't taught or don't see? The bottom line is that the community has changed. In the past, the community helped the children of weak parents; directing those children long before they got to a point of no return, and didn't wait for elected officials to jump in.

My friend and I grew up in two-family houses one block from the projects. All types of people, with all types of incomes and backgrounds lived on my block and around me. We learned to live together and rely on each other. Maybe that's the real problem. Now we are so separated we look down on one another and forget that we are really family. I believe that's what Jesus meant when He told us to love our neighbor the same way we love ourselves. In a polarized city such as ours, maybe it's time to see others who are not like you as your neighbor instead of as a threat or a problem. We are the community.

There are organizations working in our city to combat these issues. We don't need more organizations, we need more workers. Find a place where you can roll up your sleeves and help. Start with your family, your block, your neighborhood. With the help of God, we can fix our problems. We are the community.

Rev. Dr. Noel G.L. Hutchinson Jr. is pastor of First Baptist Church Lauderdale.

Facebook—The Invitation Needs to Get Lost in the Mail[x]
December 9, 2017

I'm glad that the 45th president stuck to his written speech (for the most part).[xxi] I also understand that as the sitting president he was invited to the opening of the Mississippi Civil Rights Museum in Jackson, MS, which is about a 2 1/2 hour drive from Memphis. (If another Republican president had been invited, there might be some pushback as well--I'm saying this for the historical benefit of some.)

We live in the land, supposedly, of free speech. That being said, NO president has been so reprehensible and divisive as this one. Few presidents (a very short list that includes Woodrow Wilson) have been as blatantly racist. So for these reasons I'm posting the following TODAY. Remember you heard it here FIRST.

To the National Civil Rights Museum, to Tennessee Governor Haslam, to Mayor Strickland and to any other entity doing ANYTHING surrounding the 50th anniversary of Dr. King's assassination in Memphis:

PLEASE DO NOT INVITE PRESIDENT TRUMP TO THIS ANNIVERSARY AT ALL!!!! It would be totally disrespectful to the memory of Dr. King, the millions who died in chains of servitude, their descendants, and anyone who fights for and appreciates freedom. I pray you understand this and send that invitation to someone else.
Anybody else with me on this?

Facebook—A Perspective on #metoo
November 21, 2017

Right now many accusations of inappropriate behavior, at the least, became and are becoming visible. The guilty are prominent men across demographics. Their patterns of abuse toward women are seeing daylight. The only one seemingly getting a pass in all of this is the resident in the White House, who can talk about grabbing female genitals without any recompense.

I've seen men in their frustration push back against what's happening now, thinking that women are indiscriminately targeting men after many years of apparent silence. Their feeling is that some of these women are lying because of the time lapse from when the offense (alleged, in their minds) took place until now. While that may be true in some cases, to push back against this issue is insensitive, because almost EVERY woman has had to deal with inappropriate remarks, advances, abuse, and assaults. Many others have dealt with rape – attempted and executed. Look at it this way--your sister, wife, mother, daughter, aunt, grandmother, etc…have dealt or will deal with some degree of sexual aggression or abuse at some point in her life.

My hope is that we as a society move toward fixing the landscape, so that predators – whether they prey on women or men – lose their cover.

Facebook—#metoo Close to Home: From another Perspective November 25, 2017

In the midst of the #metoo movement, and the latest rash of sexual abuse revelations, I want to tell a story that I hope will help many. It is probably more revealing than I've ever been in this medium. I'm a believer in not being exhibitionist on Facebook, for many things ought to be kept private. Yet, I think this disclosure will bless and encourage some, and educate others.

DISCLAIMER--THIS IS LONG.

Some of you who will read this knew Agnes Hutchinson, my number one shero of all time hands down. Well, during my courtship and approximately the first nine months of my marriage, my shero couldn't STAND my wife. For those of you who know my wife, you know she's a sweetheart; so much so that when it is said that someone takes issue with her, people automatically look sideways at the other person! Real talk. Well, I defended my wife while not disrespecting my mother, and I did a lot of praying.

I knew my mother better than anyone did, except for my father. Many times, in spite of age and relationship, we were more like siblings. I asked her directly what her problem was with my wife. She, my old school Jamaican mother, said, "That hair – she favor Rasta."

Understand that my mother was around during the development of Rastafarianism, which took place when she was a teenager in Kingston, so her point of reference was the real thing. I told her that Becky's twists, and later locks, were a fashion statement and not religious. "Mi no care," is the only part of her response I can print.

Many of her friends, some of whom might read this, also talked to her. A couple of them, when they checked on me, told me so. Needless to say, I did a lot of praying; and defending. To Becky's credit, she treated my mother with respect and never complained.

One day, with a little more heat, I asked my mother, "What's the problem? I love both of you. Tell me, what's the real problem? 'Cause it can't just be her hair!" The following is what happened, and why I wrote this post for your contemplation:

Sometime in my mother's late teens/early 20's, before she entered nursing school, a Rasta tried to "fool around her," a euphemism for trying to "get some" unsolicited. (NOTE: I first heard this story when I was in my 20's.) My mother told him no, and when he didn't get the message, she took matters into her own hands.

PAUSE...

For those of you reading this who knew my mother, you know that even though she was a sweetheart, she had NO PROBLEM bringing a fight to you. She was NOT the one to play with. I've seen her put burly, grown men to flight by being ready to fight (for good reason, I need to add). So, when she first told me this story, I assumed, especially by the way she told it, that the Rasta simply got on her nerves. HOWEVER, when she told me the story again in my 40's, she began shaking and crying. WHY? The Rasta tried to RAPE HER.

PAUSE...

Black women have been abused by the slave master, Black men and each other. Predators are in our families, churches and other houses of worship. Predators have also victimized boys and men. All of it is wrong, and we seldom talk about it. Let's take steps to correct it. All of it. When it isn't corrected, it infects ALL of our relationships, as evidenced by the one in this story. We also need safe spaces where we can heal from our trauma.

I held this 70-plus year old woman, my mother, as she cried. I confessed that I never realized that that was what she went through. I cried. I could feel the weight leave her shoulders. And from that moment on, she did everything to make up for how she treated Becky, starting with bugging me about her buying Becky an outfit for Christmas--something she NEVER did for anyone but me when I was younger. The two of them became close--so much so that they would gang up on me. I didn't like that part, lol.

PAUSE…

Now if you knew Agnes Hutchinson, you know there is more to this story. Remember when I said she took matters into her own hands? Well, Homeboy tried to make his move, and my mother bit into his face and chomped down to the white meat, tearing a chunk out of his flesh. She then spit it out. The next part of the story are her words, "When 'im see 'im blood, 'im run like hell!"

My shero. Love you Ma. Agnes Hutchinson. Hardcore. No joke.

Facebook—The Wide Receiver
November 3, 2017

As I go back to work, I'm reminded that it's sometimes hazardous to read the Facebook news feed, lol, for you see things that are ridiculous, sublime, or downright rude and purposely nuanced with inaccuracies. But to each his own, I guess.

I just saw something reposted that caused me to shake my head. As clergy, we are often called upon by all – from government officials to the grassroots, from CEO's to "Pookie 'n 'em." That's a part of what we do. Many people don't understand this reality, for guidance is something that we all need from time to time.

What also happens is that the people you help turn on you. I used to get upset about it, but then I remembered that as a shepherd, sheep will sometimes bite you--the one who helped them. When this happens now, I just shake my head and become sad for the person with the sharp teeth. When you constantly bite others, one day you will look up and be by yourself. I've seen it happen too many times.

I'm also writing this because I remembered something that the late Dr. Charles Thurman, a son of Clarksdale, MS, Pastor of the Second Baptist Church of Mumford, NY, and a former acting Dean of Colgate Rochester Divinity School's Program for Black Studies, said to me about 30 years ago. Want to know what he said?

Here it is:

"Son, being a preacher is like being in a football game. But, you aren't the lineman, you don't play defense, and you don't run the ball. Matter of fact you don't have any blockers. You're the wide receiver—it's just you and the Lord."

The reality of this statement helps to keep me focused and grounded. I think this may also help someone else. I live in the reality that "Greater is He who is in me, than he who is in the world."[xxii] So, I'll be the wide receiver with pride. Peace.

Facebook—Do For Self[xiii]
October 31, 2017

I attended a banquet today that was sponsored by a particular organization in Memphis that is on track to give the community a half billion dollars by the end of 2018!!! They also revealed the method by which this will be done. I was so blown away I stayed in my seat 15 minutes after the banquet was over.

The thought then hit me: *We (Black people) could do the same thing in our community on a smaller scale (because we have less resources) if we work together.* We've become so divided and ego-driven that we excel in pontification but fall down in action.

Attempts were made in the recent past with Gary Rowe and the Black United Fund (I was involved), and the Church and Community Investment Fund anchored by Drs. Fred Lofton and Charles Dinkins (my predecessor at First Baptist). I was involved with this one as well. I'm letting you know this as a witness, not a braggart. Both folded due to lack of support, and the need for those who would not join for ego satisfaction.

I'm trying to work during the rest of my life to leave a legacy that outlives me, and isn't beholden to who gets the credit and who smiles best for the camera. I pray you feel the same. If you don't, I pray that the feeling grows on you.

TIME TO GET TO WORK...

Facebook—The Power of a Word[xxiv]
October 23, 2017

Today I was reminded of how God works through simple words. I posted the following words yesterday in response to someone using the word "irreplaceable" in describing a recent, well- known, sudden death:

> *This may be too soon for some, but no one is irreplaceable. It simply means that it's time for the rest of us to step up and get to work. It's called a wake-up call. Now let's emulate this great example.*

John Best, along with some of you, saw these words. They caused him to act. After he got permission from the widow of Bernal Smith, he, along with many in-studio guests and callers, spent this afternoon and evening talking about the life and legacy of brother Smith on 88.5 FM. When he told me I was the catalyst for that undertaking, I was blown away. Still am.

All because of some words.

Words have power. They can heal. Give strength. Hurt. Wound. Kill.

The Bible talks about the power of the tongue, and one of the things that God hates are those who "sow discord among the brethren."[xxv] You sow discord with words.
Make sure you use your words wisely, and give credit to the beginning of thought and wisdom – Almighty God.
Peace.

Facebook—Do They Have the Right? Can You See Their Point? October 11, 2017

There are people whose opinions I respect outside of Facebook who say that since the NFL players were hired to do a job, they should adhere to the instructions to not protest by bended knee.[xxvi] These are good, "respectable" Black folk sharing this perspective.

Well, I guess all of the work of unions should have passed us by, and we should dwell in the land of sweatshops. We should just be grateful to have a job, under any conditions.

The First Amendment gives us the right to protest, and in this case, the protest isn't against the flag, but against the decimation of life in a particular community--ours! So, NFL, according to you, the workers who make up 72% of your workforce should be seen, worked to a future life of chronic illness, and not heard.

To you who continue to say the NFL players should be silent, especially if you share their ethnicity, I have one question: Do you do the "Stepin Fetchit" much?

Facebook—What is Reconciliation? October 3, 2017

I'm taking a break from serious work to make this observation. It was prompted by someone who posted in one of my threads (the name is omitted to protect the guilty, lol).

What is reconciliation? Often, I'll hear some Christian white people say that black and white people need reconciliation. Most times, they mean that we, Black folk, need to unite with them while forgiving them. Notice that there is no recompense to us for damages caused by them. That's why some denominations can apologize for their role in slavery with freeness, but have trouble denouncing racist institutions.

Don't understand? Here's an example. In seminary, we were learning about the Black church. One student, a white woman, said, "There should be no white church or black church--why don't you (talking about Black churches) join together with us?" Some of my classmates got nervous, and then looked at me (I went to a PWI seminary in New Jersey). I calmly asked, "Well, if we do what you suggest, who's gonna be in charge?" I never got an answer.

The chicken, when talking to the pig, always wants reconciliation for breakfast. That's because for the chicken it's an offering; but for the pig, it's a sacrifice.
Somebody will get that on the way home.

Facebook—How to Slay "isms"
October 2, 2017

To me, there exists a three-legged stool that is the anchor of forward motion and the solution to our 'isms. Many are familiar with one of its legs, which is protest. When injustice is present, protest exposes it. It is necessary in many situations. Black Lives Matter, the removal of Confederate monuments and other protests, for example, brought light to situations that may have stayed covered up. The 60's protests in Selma and Birmingham did the same thing.

The second leg is policy. Protest should always work in some way with policy, or those who are the focus of the protest will ignore it, or, as with the NFL, change the protest in an attempt to remove its sting. Laws ensure that right practices and protections exist.

However, there is a third leg that we overlook to our peril. It is spirituality. Not misguided spirituality that allows people to go to church while beating down and abusing others. Remember, white supremacists attend church, and their theology teaches hate. Let's look at the 45th president, for example. He will be in Las Vegas on Wednesday, two days after the heinous shooting that took place in a local night club. Yet, he is scheduled to go to Puerto Rico the day before, almost three weeks after Hurricane Maria created a situation there of cataclysmic proportions. Today, the one who misquotes Bible books sounded like the "Passa-in-Chief" because of a decently written speech.
Without right-guided spirituality, public policy doesn't change. Without right-guided spirituality, lawmakers

continuously attempt to dismantle a healthcare bill and remove coverage for up to 30 million Americans while simultaneously putting healthcare out of reach cost-wise for many more. Make no mistake, when your spiritual walk is out of whack, you have no cares for anyone but yourself. Think about this as you observe what is happening in our nation.

I need to pray. Prayer then changes me. As I change, my life becomes a witness and a blessing to others, and people will see that I truly know God.

Facebook—A Mass Shooting and a Sincere Prayer
October 2, 2017

Vegas...Lord have much mercy.
You may not agree, but mental health challenges and overall wickedness is real:

For our struggle is not against flesh and blood, but against the rulers, against the authorities, against the powers of this dark world and against the spiritual forces of evil in the heavenly realms (Ephesians 6:12, NIV).

Lord,

Deliver us from the callousness toward life, in whatever community it is in. Deliver us from the wickedness of white supremacy. Deliver us from the lack of conflict resolution. Deliver us and help us with healing from misdirected rage and mental illness. Deliver us and help us when we are in the midst of lament and frustration. We need you in this season, O God. Help us in our understanding and misunderstanding. Help us where we can agree, and where we disagree. Change our hardened hearts. Soothe our wounded spirits.

In Jesus' name,

Amen.

Facebook—Charlottesville—I Couldn't Take It
August 13, 2017

I've been in travel mode for the past day, and I'm still digesting what happened in Charlottesville VA. Back at the turn of the 20th century, the KKK wore sheets, partially to hide their identity. Today, they don't give a damn whether you know who they are or not. Notice the reason for their protest – they don't want to be left out or left behind. Well Mr. Racist, your fellow white man is to blame for that one. Matter of fact, the one you helped elect is the same one attempting to relieve you of your healthcare. Yet your aim is toward black and brown people, along with liberal whites. It takes low intelligence with a substantial mixture of racism to miss the mark that 'bigly'.

To the white person reading this, it's time to speak up and speak out against this, and all, neo-Nazi, KKK behavior. Stop hiding in the land of the silent majority. That's how Hitler was able to succeed with his madness.

To the Black apologists for everything white---wake the hell up! Period. Yes, the language is strong, but for the sickness you have, a strong remedy is needed.
To the rest of us who aren't already active, "Wake up everybody, no more sleeping in bed…"[xxvii]
Peace.

Facebook—Fake Is as Fake Does
August 3, 2017

I've been told that I'm a straight shooter, and that many people read this page. Several who never comment have told me that they appreciate what I say, and, as happened yesterday, several news people also see what I write ;-). Many say that I'm quite blunt. If you REALLY knew me (few on here do), you would know that I COULD be worse, lol!

In that spirit, let me be serious and candid (I also have a sarcastic sense of humor--pray for me). I'm praying for the modern-day male and female "profit prophets" who have a WERD without study, and who are so ready to correct every ill of the Church because God only gave *them* the answer.

The Church has existed for over 2,000 years, yet you say that it can't make it and won't get right without your guidance. Then you will talk to those who have responsibilities and/or pastor in the church --mind you, you've not even pastored one yourself--like they're beneath you, and rebuke them for what you say they're doing wrong. Well, take a break from inhaling too much of yourself and read these words from the Jesus you say you represent:

> *Do not judge, or you too will be judged. For in the same way you judge others, you will be judged, and with the measure you use, it will be measured to you. "Why do you look at the speck of sawdust in your brother's eye and pay no attention to the plank in your own eye? How can you say to your brother, 'Let me take the speck out of your eye,' when all the time there is a plank in your own eye? You hypocrite, first*

> *take the plank out of your own eye, and then you will see clearly to remove the speck from your brother's eye* (Matthew 7:1-5 NIV).

Now, many of us, yours truly included, have jumped into God's work ready to make a difference, thinking that we have the answers. But just as God had to tell Elijah that there were 7,000 prophets who hadn't bowed to Baal, I'm telling you God is still right. I'm definitely not God, but this humble word is your similar notice.

Translation--God is watching your foolishness and judging you the way you judge others. Check yourself before you wreck yourself.

Peace.

Facebook—A Perspective on Thanksgiving
November 24, 2016

This is indeed a day to be thankful. Don't focus on the mythology that helped to culturally shape this day—that the Native Americans helped the Pilgrims to have a successful harvest, and they got together to have a Thanksgiving meal. That story ended with reservations and was buried by the current struggle out in the West to prevent a pipeline which would pollute water sources. The children of those Native Americans at Plymouth now face water hoses like the ones African-Americans faced in Birmingham back in the '60's. Pray for that situation, and, if led, do what you can to help.

Instead, focus on how good God has been to you. Focus on the fellowship that awaits you where you will eat today. Revel in the love of family. Enjoy the one you're with. Thank God for your church family if you have one. Above all, use today to focus on how blessed you really are, despite challenges. And may God be praised!
Happy Thanksgiving.

Facebook—What Should You Do When your "Good" is Abused?
November 4, 2016

> *Let us not become weary in doing good, for at the proper time we will reap a harvest if we do not give up. Therefore, as we have opportunity, let us do good to all people, especially to those who belong to the family of believers* (Galatians 6:9-10).

I post this today for those who need to see it. I was reminded by someone yesterday that I've been overly generous in my support of others and their causes. Then when it was my turn for support, many of the ones I've helped walked away. Others twisted their knives into my back, thinking I didn't see what they did or feel the pain.

What keeps me going is the knowledge of two things. First, I do it because it's right. There is no need for others to suffer because of one or two. Second, God is watching and wants me to live up to the Scripture cited above. Then, God, overlooking my own faults, will give me the harvest that others withhold.

Facebook—Focus on the Real Thing
August 24, 2016

I read a reliable story about those trained to identify real money from counterfeit. In training, they are never exposed to that which is fake, but only to what is real. The counterfeit is then easy to spot.

Many of you on Facebook, including those who profess to know Jesus in a personal way, are now very concerned about pastors who make 800 times what people in their communities make, and whom Creflo Dollar says God told him to vote for. Some of you want to hold clergy – probably all of us – accountable for what the guilty have done.

I have a better idea. Don't throw out Jesus with the bathwater. Don't say that all clergy are counterfeit. And especially don't say, "I didn't mean you, you're one of the good ones." That's even more insulting. It's like calling me and like-minded individuals "Puff the magical Negro." See my point?

Just do like those trained to spot real money. When you find it, keep it. To use another analogy, understand that you eat meat and throw away bones. Then do like Eddie Kendricks and "Keep on truckin' baby…"[xxviii]

Peace.

Facebook—Do Black Lives Matter to Black People?
November 17, 2015

It's interesting to me that no group of people gets judged by the actions of one or two like people of African descent. Let one or more do something crazy or disrespectful and it becomes a reason for Black lives not to matter. Let hundreds of white students turn over cars after a football game, or shoot up a movie theatre, and the behavior is localized to the guilty, not the entire race. A young white man kills nine Black people in a church, and when caught says he's hungry and gets taken to Burger King; a young Black man with a bb gun is shot before he has a chance to drop his toy.

What makes this even worse is that BLACK PEOPLE buy into the myth of the respectable Negro (If we act with respect, we will get respect in return). If you've been paying attention at all, that doesn't work. Ask the young man in North Carolina who was shot to death when his car broke down and he was asking for help. Ask the drummer in Florida who was killed on the highway while waiting for a tow truck. Ask Dr. Marcia Bowden, a local doctor, who was on her way to respond to an emergency, and wound up in jail and then the emergency room.

Yes, we should train our youth. Yes, several of us should do better. Yes, those of us who are guilty should stop killing our people. Yes, disgraceful behavior is just that--a disgrace. But Black lives matter. The problem is, many of us don't believe it.

Facebook—If You're Asleep, You're Already Calm – Time to Wake Up and Get to Work[xxix] *November 4, 2015*

Let me put my foot on the gas and say something that may get some of you upset. Quite frankly, I don't much care. Pay attention.

First, Memphis has been in such a deep sleep that we have no fear of people NOT being calm and tearing up property as a result of no indictment from the Grand Jury. The same naysayers, talk show hosts, and Facebook prognosticators ain't tearing nothing up but adding more conversation. So, to my fellow clergy, no need to worry about people being calm. Those who are asleep are calm. Let's try to constructively wake them up. [xxx]

Second, rightly or wrongly, it's preacher bashing season. Many – especially those who should KNOW BETTER – are bashing those who have been working in this area. Guess what? These same preachers (with a couple of notable exceptions) you've been frying are a main part of the reason why this issue didn't die. They put major pressure on the DA to the point that she felt "bullied."

What is my point? The church is a part of the solution, and just because you don't like it, it won't change this fact. Stop worrying about Rev'un Chickenfat, he ain't a part of this. And stop saying we should go home. YOU go home. We can do things and yield influence in ways that are needed right now, and many of us will use our clout wisely.

Finally, this is really OUR work. It's gonna take the Grassroots Coalition, the Nation of Islam, the lawyers for the Stewart family, United Against Violence 901, AND THE COMMUNITY to make this work. All of us must work at our levels for this to work. And no, stop trying to get to the front of the line to be Dr. King. Work. And for those of you with conversation but no action..............we will see you at the finish line after the work gets done; after you say you were there all along.

--Management

Drops mic.

Facebook—What about the Haters?
November 14, 2014

In the modern cultural conversation, there is a word that receives too much focus. That word is "haters." People talk about it; even gospel songs sometimes focus on it. However, what does the Bible say about it? This is an important question, for many on Facebook using the word 'hater' claim to have a relationship with Jesus, and others claim some level of spirituality.

> *Do not fret because of evil men or be envious of those who do wrong; for like the grass they will soon wither, like green plants they will soon die away* (Psalm 37:1-2).
> *You prepare a table before me in the presence of my enemies. You anoint my head with oil; my cup overflows* (Psalm 23:5).

Translation: If you do anything beyond breathing, you will have haters. They will come, and they will go. God will sometimes either put you, or allow you to be, in the midst of them; but God will also allow you to feast as they watch you eat and be blessed. Remember, they can't sit AT the table, they can only watch you.

The moral of this story: Live right, stop talking and worrying about haters, and leave the heavy lifting to God. I hope these words help you and set you free.

Peace

Facebook—How to Survive Piranhas
October 30, 2015

I'm posting the following for the sake of those reading this who need encouragement. If you know Jesus, remember you are to be the light of the world, designed to attract others to Him. What does that mean? Live by the wheat and tares principle.

There are always going to be people in your life who are hangers-on, attracted to your light and wanting to take advantage of you, and it. Some will brag that they know you. Still others, thinking you can't see them for what they are, or taking advantage of your kindness, will ride on your generosity. After they get to where they think they can by using you, they abandon you. We often talk about shaking people loose out of our lives. I suggest that you leave them alone. Why?

Well, if you truly exude light, they need to learn by watching you, and seeing Christ in you. Let Jesus, who really knows how to judge, watch your back while you continue to live your witness. The seed that others sow, when it fully develops, will either bless or choke them. The judgment of them is beyond your pay grade – that's God's business.
So yes, I know there are some who are hangers-on. Yes, I also know there are others who think I can't "see" them. Yes, that's life. But I've lived long enough to see God move so strong against those who schemed against me that it caused me to have a holy fear.

I'm not saying all of this to say that I'm all that, but to encourage you today and remind you that if you know the

Lord, God has your back. Look past the sea of piranhas you may be in right now, and trust God. Let God handle who should stay and who should leave. You keep your focus on the Lord.

New and Context Driven Ways to Reach the Masses
March 22, 2015

This week, I saw an interesting short video. The setting was a high school in the 'hood, where the students gather in the school auditorium for an assembly. A rapper sits down at a piano and, after playing a well-executed arpeggio, explains how at one time he would write complex lyrics to go with the melody, but for this occasion he chose to keep things simple and pro-Black so they, the students, would get the message. For the next minute and a half we take a sonic ride through a series of common sense chants laid over a catchy beat, which are one part humorous and two parts profane. They range from "read a book," to "brush your teeth;" "wear deodorant" to "raise your kids;" and "your body needs water" to "buy some land." It gave a very basic but powerful message.[xxxi]

As much as I appreciated the message, I also knew I couldn't spread it. The context in which I serve—this church—doesn't need a powerful, yet very basic message like this strewn over a verbal bed of multisyllabic cuss words. For many of us, the message would get drowned out by the profanity. Yet this method does raise an interesting question: Do we need to use more effective methods to reach those around us? I would dare say that some who would watch the video might have someone in their lives to give this type of advice to. However, without meeting them halfway, they may never hear it.

We as the Church are called upon to reach the masses. In the age in which we live, we must find impactful ways to reach them where they are, without confusing them about our witness. In that spirit, we are about to embark upon an innovative journey that, I believe, will be a great watershed moment in our collective history. In a few weeks, we will begin an online Bible study. What does this mean? Many people, and several of you, no longer come to a physical location for Bible study. There are several reasons why this might be the case. One is probably the increased busyness of modern life. Another is the desire for a setting where Biblical and life questions can be asked and answered without fear of embarrassment. Still another is the erosion of reading levels in our society, such that students would need a setting where they could learn, if necessary, at their own pace.

Through the use of the church's Facebook page and my personal webpage, www.noelhutchinson.com, we will periodically host Bible study online. To my knowledge, it has not been done in the way you will see it here. Later in the year, after we upgrade our church's website, we will also host our Bible study there. This Bible study is for the unchurched who are curious about the things of God, as well as youth, young adults, and anyone with questions and a thirst to learn more.[xxxii]

Of course, this is something that WE must do, and I will need your help in making this work. I will produce the videos and post them. Those of you on social media have probably seen the first promo for this study. Spread it among your friends. Talk about it with those you know. If you know how to download it, share it through email. For those of you who don't know the foreign land that is social media and the internet, ask your children or grandchildren to pull it up on Facebook so you can see it and they can watch it with you. This is a way for all of us to get involved with evangelism and Christian education at the ground level. When we do this, we will live the words of this great hymn:

How to reach the masses, men of every birth,
For an answer, Jesus gave the key:
"And I, if I be lifted up from the earth,
Will draw all men unto Me."[xxxiii]

Let's all be about the business of using this 21st century method to "Lift Him Up."

CHAPTER FIVE - THE CHRISTIAN LIFE AND YOU

What You Believe Makes Choices for You
June 19, 2016

About a week ago a man, seemingly having issues with his sexual identity while simultaneously identifying with Islamic extremists, shot up a nightclub in Orlando. Fifty people lie dead, while fifty-three others reside between minor injuries and waving at the Church Triumphant.

Several quick things come to mind while viewing this incident. First, the media's shaping of it as the second worst mass shooting in United States history is a rewrite of history. Unfortunately, the DNA of our land is bathed in violence, much of it suffered by us and Native American peoples. Second, to be a Christian implies that one understands that those who disagree with your worldview shouldn't be marked for death. If we employ the practice of "death for sins," real or perceived, we would depopulate the earth. To be clear- those who target gays and abortion clinics with violence may have heard of Jesus, but haven't met Him.

Watching this event unfold shows the importance of theology. Simply put, theology is the description of who God is and how God interacts with us. It often influences and shapes one's ideology, or personal belief system. When your theology becomes skewed to the point where it solely focuses on you while allowing you to abuse others, it is cultic and flawed; thus encouraging a warped ideology. Everyone, whether religious or not, lives by a personal theology, or ideology if used in a purely secular sense. Why is this important? Ideology is the strongest force in the world; for once a person anchors in an ideology, not only will they not be moved, but they will recruit and raise up others to embrace their way of thinking. We have seen this scenario play out in history time and time again.

Knowing this should cause us to anchor even more in God's Word, rightly dividing the Word of truth. Please consider these words: well-shaped theology contributes to a well-shaped life, and one that isn't in the headlines for the wrong reasons.

Some Effects of Sin
April 23, 1995

Many of you, by this time, have heard the terrible news from Oklahoma City. As of this writing, 52 people have died, 400 are injured and 150 are unaccounted for. A collective cry of anguish has gone up around the globe as we wonder what kind of heartless person could execute this heinous crime.

In the book of Matthew, chapter 24, verses 6 through 13, we see the following: *And ye shall hear of wars and rumours of wars: see that ye be not troubled: for all these things must come to pass, but the end is not yet. For nation shall rise against nation, and kingdom against kingdom: and there shall be famines, and pestilences, and earthquakes, in divers places. All these are the beginning of sorrows. Then shall they deliver you up to be afflicted, and shall kill you: and ye shall be hated of all nations for my name's sake. And then shall many be offended, and shall betray one another, and shall hate one another. And many false prophets shall rise, and shall deceive many. And because iniquity shall abound, the love of many shall wax cold. But he that shall endure unto the end, the same shall be saved* (KJV). Understand that these words of Jesus point to an unfortunate reality; more tragic events, like the one in Oklahoma City, will probably take place in the future.

The Bible has a timeless, three letter critique for this kind of activity: sin. The word sin is not a popular one these days. We like to blame societal factors on many things, such as economic inequality, racism and sexism. This observation is accurate, but incomplete. The lowest common denominator to all these societal situations is **sin**.

Today's message partially investigates the reality of, and answer to sin. The basic definition is missing the mark of God's standards of holiness and perfection, due to initial disobedience on the part of humankind. This is a standard that eludes the grasp of all. Recognize that because of sin, the church will never be out of business. Men and women, despite racial, social or economic status, will always need to be set free from sin. As we go out and make disciples, we will become a great part of societal solutions. When we present the solution to sin, we will deal with societal factors that in reality are the symptoms of sin. The solution for sin is in relationship with Jesus Christ, for He has already made up the gap in whom we should be versus how we fall short. Our encouragement is knowing that as we bear witness to the power of Christ, He will be with us. Remember, greater is He who is in us than he who is in the world.

God Works in Spite of Us
October 22, 1995

By the time you read this, the Million Man March will be a part of history, good or bad. In spite of its intentions, the reality of local problems in cities across this nation remains. In our city over the past week, a grocer shot a man in front of his son. This took place at a location not far from our church. Many other tragedies will continue to happen and be paraded in the media ad nauseam. The operative question confronting us should be, "Will we just vent frustrations in a large public forum and return to business as usual, or will we try a proactive approach?"

When Israel gathered on their Day of Atonement, it was with the understanding that they would make a continued lifestyle commitment to God. The Day of Atonement signaled for them the reality of their imperfection in the sight of a perfect and holy God. Our community should, at this point, rally around each other and rebuild. This effort should note that our ultimate victory will come from God.

Two obstacles, however, stand in the way. First, we must realize that we, as African-Americans, are not a monolithic community. African-Americans are the descendants of various African ethnic groups who, through slavery, have been placed together for better or worse. Because of this, those who perform noble, consensus building work in our community should persevere; the bandwagon will eventually become connected to the towing vehicle. Second, I am convinced that the only lasting change in our communities will come through the bride of Christ, the church. Our history in this country reinforces this fact. Some in our community may doubt our validity, but we are the only hope.

It is interesting that God has entrusted this sacred plan to fallible human beings. Yet, in spite of us, people continue to find the way to Jesus, and the church continues to march on. Praise the Lord!

A Perspective on Viewing Religion
March 17, 1996

As we focus our preaching efforts this Lenten season on prayer, we should take a brief look at how religion is impacting and being impacted by society. Many of us have followed the court case in Mississippi concerning school prayer with great interest. In addition, we looked on as the NBA wrestled with a player who refused to stand during our National Anthem due to religious conviction.

Interesting information has surfaced during the court case on prayer. It is alleged that a person was paid by a group of churches to conduct a Christian class in a public school. Furthermore, it appears that this teacher, as well as certain other the public-school teachers, showed intolerance toward non-Christians. In the case of the NBA player, it is interesting that the issue of allegiance has come up when the basketball season is two-thirds complete.

How should we view these proceedings? As Baptists, we have traditionally believed in the separation of church and state. This is for two reasons. First, the Baptist witness developed during a time of religious and national tyranny; it was perilous in medieval England and Western Europe to be a part of a denomination that was not sponsored and sanctioned by the state. Baptists, in the genesis of our witness, felt that true expression and conviction should be unfettered by state interference; it is subject only to God. In light of the Christian Coalition and the right to life proponents, this is interesting conversation. They seek to legislate morality, or, to put it another way, make the unconverted live as if they were Christian. We know that this is impossible, for you cannot live the Christian life solely under your own power; it takes the grand assistance of the Holy Spirit, which unbelievers cannot have. Second, we must be change agents from within society through our witness. It is a witness that intersects society through *proclamation* and *lifestyle*. We must boldly speak out against injustice, and live a life that mirrors Christ to the world.

As we embrace our mission as Christians, let us gain strength and conviction from the following words of Jesus:

Ye are the salt of the earth: but if the salt have lost his savour, wherewith shall it be salted? it is thenceforth good for nothing, but to be cast out, and to be trodden under foot of men. Ye are the light of the world. A city that is set on an hill cannot be hid. Neither do men light a candle, and put it under a bushel, but on a candlestick; and it giveth light unto all that are in the house. Let your light so shine before men, that they may see your good works, and glorify your Father which is in heaven (Matthew 5:13-16 KJV).

God Should be the Center of Our Lives
July 21, 1996

Many of us have travelled, or will travel, during the course of this summer. 20th century developments, such as the automobile and the airplane, have made travel quick and convenient. We move frequently in and out of airports, train and bus stations, and cars. Our journeys have taken us to family reunions, conventions, and on vacations. We assume that when we and our family members travel, everyone will reach their destination safely. Although recent developments show us that our normal assumptions should never apply, this should not make us worry, or cause us to be leery of travel. These developments should remind us of who ultimately is in control. God alone holds the keys of safe passage and security.

We are often guilty of making God a trivial, convenient part of our lives. God is only considered when we have "an itch that needs to be scratched." We often forget that at all times and in all places, we need God. Humankind, at this point, can merely make an attempt to harness the physical realities of a world that God fully controls. When we place our destiny in God's hands, we have indeed put it in the right place.

There is an example of this on Calvary. Jesus, upon finishing the task of dying for the sins of the world – past, present, and future – gave His spirit to the Father. Jesus knew He needed a proper custodian of that which was vital until He had need of it again. As we travel and find ourselves in the daily course of our business, let us remember to put all things in God's hands.

Do Any of Us Possess the Keys to Hell?
October 6, 1996

On Wednesday, September 25, 1996, the *Commercial Appeal*, in its editorial section, ran a piece by Jeff Jacoby, a columnist for the *Boston Globe*, under the caption, "Compassion for a Cold-blooded Killer." Jacoby recounted the final hours of Raymond Lee Stewart, a man executed for killing six people in a Rockford, Illinois grocery store in January of 1981. Right before his execution, Cardinal Joseph Bernardin of the Archdiocese of Chicago spent some time with Stewart, and prayed for him. Mr. Jacoby took issue with this, saying that Cardinal Bernardin, who is terminally ill, should spend his last days concerned for those who are good, instead of the cruel, like Stewart. Jacoby says, "A society is far down the road to decay when its religious leaders show as much tenderness to murderers and rapists as to their victims. Compassion to everyone amounts to compassion for no one."[xxxiv] Jacoby even quotes Scripture in making his argument!

Mr. Jacoby happens to be like many people who are on the outside looking in at the life of those committed to Christ. When we view how Jesus dealt with the thief on the cross, we see genuine compassion. This compassion in action assured the thief a place in glory that day. However, this compassion did not remove the thief from paying the price for his misdeeds. The woman caught "in the very act" of adultery was told by Jesus to *go and sin no more* (John 8:11). Compassion, whether extended to the saint or the sinner, is always appropriate.

We must realize that God hates our sin. Sin is what keeps us separated from God. Thank God, Jesus Christ came, bled, died and rose from the dead; creating a bridge to the Father. Because of this, when God sees we who have a relationship with Christ, God sees the blood of Christ. Until life is extinguished by the hands of death, there always exists the possibility of reconciliation with God.

Mr. Jacoby should be grateful that there are religious leaders who are willing to show compassion to those at the fringes of society. If more of us would do it, we would begin to make major dents in the cycle of self-destruction that permeates our society. More jails, alongside the death penalty, are not the answer. Twenty years of a booming penal industry has shown us that. Privatization of jails is not the answer; this will be the 21st century's version of sharecropping. The answer is found in genuine, Christ-centered compassion, which ultimately leads the lost to faith in Jesus. We must be the examples and bearers of these truths.

U-Turns are Possible
April 20, 1997

Two items riveted my attention this past week. On Wednesday, I watched *Primetime Live* with the rest of America as Sammy "The Bull" Gravano was interviewed by Dianne Sawyer. I have been aware, as many among us, of organized crime's influence on the quality of life. Mr. Gravano spoke to this, and about the process of formally becoming a gangster—a "made man." Each made man was to swear to put the Cosa Nostra before God, family and country. He was then told that if his son was on his deathbed dying of cancer, and the Cosa Nostra ("The Family") had need of him, he was to <u>immediately</u> leave his son's bedside and do what the family said. Interesting, to say the least. Sammy "The Bull" Gravano went on to execute 19 people, including mob boss Paul Castellano.

The second item was in Thursday's *Commercial Appeal.* In the appeal section, a day in 1972 was relived in which a young Vietnamese girl, whose clothes were burned off by napalm, ran from her village toward an Associated Press photographer. The village was being bombed by American forces, who were told that it contained no civilians. A picture of this young girl became, for many, one of the most memorable scenes of the Vietnam War. The commanding officer saw the picture the next day over breakfast and it haunted him for years, eventually contributing to his alcoholism and divorce.

These two examples deal with conflict, tension, and a host of other moral and spiritual issues. Ultimately, they bring the three main subjects--Mr. Gravano, the young Vietnamese girl, and the commanding officer--into a necessary look at redemption. Mr. Gravano, who, admittedly, is not a true good Samaritan, nevertheless made possible the conviction of mob boss John Gotti. The commanding officer, now a United Methodist pastor; and the Vietnamese girl, now a 33-year-old Christian woman, finally met and embraced last November 11th at the Vietnam Veterans Memorial. He cried and asked for forgiveness; she readily forgave.

One of the greatest blessings from the gospel is that God allows those who have purposely driven the wrong way, gotten lost and run out of gas to make U-turns, and become filled with the everlasting fuel of Living Water. This is another reason for our joy, and for us to have hope in the midst of the world's condition.

The Importance of Fellowship
October 4, 1998

A week ago Saturday we experienced a marvelous community event. After some years, we once again had our church picnic. To paraphrase one of our members, "the weatherman cooperated," the food was delectable, the fellowship superb, the attendance outstanding, and a good time was had by all. The church, while about the business of life transformation, must take time out for fellowship. Fellowship is the glue that holds together relationships and communities.

Today is the first Sunday in October, and the apostle Paul, in a text related to both fellowship and the Lord's Supper, understood how proper fellowship gives strength to the body of Christ. Beginning in 1 Corinthians 11:17, Paul talks about distorted fellowship appearing in the church. In verse 20, Paul deals in specifics: *When you come together, it is not the Lord's Supper you eat, for as you eat, each of you goes ahead without waiting for anybody else. One remains hungry, another gets drunk.*

Paul later begins to discuss the significance of the Lord's Supper. He concludes by showing the link between good fellowship and right relationship with God in verses 27-34 as follows: *For whenever you eat this bread and drink this cup, you proclaim the Lord's death until he comes. Therefore, whoever eats the bread or drinks the cup of the Lord in an unworthy manner will be guilty of sinning against the body and blood of the Lord. A man ought to examine himself before he eats of the bread and drinks of the cup. For anyone who eats and drinks without recognizing the body of the Lord eats and drinks judgment on himself. That is why many among you are weak and sick, and a number of you have fallen asleep. When we are judged by the Lord, we are being disciplined so that we will not be condemned with the world. So then, my brothers, when you come together to eat, wait for each other. If anyone is hungry, he should eat at home, so that when you meet together it may not result in judgment.*

We have been told that self-examination concerning the Lord's Supper is necessary before we take it. This is important and is implied by this text. A greater message, however, is the connection between fellowship and Christian witness. It is obvious that there were those who could not provide their own bread and fruit of the vine for the Lord's Supper. There were also those who could overindulge themselves but would not share with others. Thus, the power and symbol of togetherness was rendered ineffective. The purpose of the Lord's Supper, besides being an ordinance and a reminder of what Christ did for us, is to strengthen the community through fellowship. Let us insure that our fellowship is pleasing to God, and our community will strengthen itself.

A Taste of the Heavenly Celebration
October 25, 1998

This past Wednesday I had an experience that will resonate with me for quite a while. Leaving First Baptist after an important meeting, I made my way to Gospel Temple Baptist Church to catch part of the annual session of the Tennessee Baptist Missionary and Educational State Convention. It had been a long, arduous day and while on the way to the church, I seriously contemplated going straight home. I pulled my car into an overflowing parking lot, and had to back out and park a block away. As I walked to the church, I was reminded of how tired I was. I got to the top of the long stairway, opened the outside door of the church, and walked into the vestibule.

What happened next was amazing. The ushers saw me through the plate glass doors leading into the sanctuary. They began to get excited and stood up almost to a person. They then beckoned for me to come inside. I looked behind me to see whom they wanted, and I was the only one in the vestibule, so I stepped forward. As soon as I entered the sanctuary music began to play. The choir began to sing, "Lord, I'm running, trying to make a hundred, for 99½ won't do." The worship service abruptly stopped and people stood and started cheering. Everyone began to look directly at me! Several people told me, "Congratulations!" The President of the State Convention, Dr. Herman Powell, asked me to come to the pulpit. I was expecting, I guess, from this fanfare, the keys to a brand-new car. The elaborate display over me was due to a goal set by the

Convention, which was unknown to me at the time. They sought to have at least 100 men in worship, and, yes, I was number 100!

In Luke, chapter 15, verses 4-7, Jesus was accused of hanging out with riffraff. His response was instructive: *Suppose one of you has a hundred sheep and loses one of them. Does he not leave the ninety-nine in the open country and go after the lost sheep until he finds it? And when he finds it, he joyfully puts it on his shoulders and goes home. Then he calls his friends and neighbors together and says, `Rejoice with me; I have found my lost sheep.' I tell you that in the same way there will be more rejoicing in heaven over one sinner who repents than over ninety-nine righteous persons who do not need to repent.*

The Lord gave me a glimpse on Wednesday of what heaven is like when a sinner begins his or her walk with Jesus Christ. There are still those who need for the heavenly hosts to have a party in their honor. We must therefore prepare to spread the good news. This portion of Scripture reminds us how important and pleasing this is to God.

Who is a Christian?
January 21, 2000

The news this past week has been eventful. By the time you read this, the nomination of John Ashcroft for Attorney General should be definitively decided. Many pundits, pro and con, have evaluated his record and shared their opinions about his confirmation. In turn, this confirmation hearing has garnered more attention than almost anything else on the eve of the presidential inauguration.

This confirmation hearing also raises a deeper, fundamental issue: What is a Christian? This should be a simple question, but when you cut through the rhetoric you will see interesting trends. People on both sides of the fence evaluated Ashcroft on how he would bring his religious faith to bear while enforcing the law. There are some that see their Christian witness and its application in life as inseparable. There are Christians who are Republicans, and others who are Democrats. Finally, there are those who wish to use their witness to legislate a national moral lifestyle.

There should be two barometers used when viewing the Christian witness. One, Christians will have differences of opinion in viewing current events. Many times in our multicultural society, viewing an event has more to do with where we stand in terms of class and ethnicity. There are Christians who favor Ashcroft and those who do not. More often than not, this exists due to our innate ability as humans to not view life from another's perspective. The second barometer involves recognizing the proper role of the church in society. Several people wish to see government as a theocracy. The Church, in this setting, would operate similar to a state church, where it would determine the morality of society.

Christians are called upon to change society through the presentation and *living* of the gospel, not the *legislation* of it. Our ability to live the Christian life is through the power of the Holy Spirit. People who are not Christians cannot live as Christians, because the Holy Spirit is only available to those who belong to Christ. Here is what Jesus says about this issue in John 14:16-17: *And I will pray the Father, and he shall give you another Comforter, that he may abide with you for ever; [Even] the Spirit of truth; whom the world cannot receive, because it seeth him not, neither knoweth him: but ye know him; for he dwelleth with you, and shall be in you* (KJV).

Living a legislated witness without power then becomes a burdensome, restrictive, and shackled chore, because you're playing an unwanted role without a script or direction. So it is left up to us who know Jesus to change the world through the Bible instead of a manufactured use of the ballot. Knowing this, imagine what would happen if we decided to live the gospel, instead of legislate or pontificate about it.

Where Can We Find Hope?
April 23, 2000

Every living being needs hope, and when hope is extinguished, life ends. For some of us, this may mean that we simply exist, similar to zombies in horror movies. This is the state of many in our society. This is what causes wanderlust in some marriages, self-destruction by drugs and riotous living, and communal dysfunction. We as humanity have taken on the job of setting our own course and predicting our fate, yet the unpredictable continues to meet us and, as the young folks say, "rock our world."

Yet, there is an antidote to hopelessness. It does not make wars and suffering go away, and it will not turn us into instant millionaires. It does not promise to cause spouses or children to act right. It does not promise us a carefree life. This antidote will change our lives so that we have a hope for life and a hope for heaven. I speak of salvation, which was purchased on Calvary and consummated on Easter.

"He is risen" are three of the most powerful words in the world. Jesus Christ entered and left the world on His own terms that we might engage this thing known as hope. Sometimes hope appears to be lost in the maze of life. Imagine, however, a world bereft of hope. Burglar alarms and "little buddy" would be useless. However, through the hope consummated by Jesus 2000 years ago, all things are possible.

As you read this, you may face challenges that appear to be insurmountable. The very anchor of your hope seems challenged. I encourage you to look backward, and then look forward. Look backward to all of the times God navigated your steps. Remember how God put you where you are today. Then, look forward. Your tomorrow is brighter because of what Jesus did on this day by asking death about His knockout punch, and the grave about His ticker tape parade.

Necessary Nuggets about the Church: What is the Church, and Why Do We Need It?
June 29, 2014

Today begins a series in the "Shepherd's Staff" titled, "Necessary Nuggets about the Church." We begin today by raising two important questions: What is the Church, and why do we need it? Harper's Bible Dictionary tells us that the word "church" is the English translation of the Greek word "ekklēsia," meaning "assembly" or "gathering." It first was the name for the global body of Christians, and has also been used to describe all the people of faith in a city, or those who worship in a particular house or local body.

Jesus considers the Church to be a part of His body, of which He is the head (John 15:1-11; 1 Corinthians 12:12, 27; Romans 12:4-5; Ephesians. 1:22-23; 4:15-16; Colossians. 1:18; 2:19), and it is His possession that will exist until the end of time (Matthew 16:18). In viewing these Biblical images it is clear that if we understand the basic definition of the Church, this should cause us to draw closer to Christ and our fellow Christians. The very word "church" suggests that we are a group, a gathering, held together in the body of Christ by our relationship with Jesus, and the complementary nature of our differing spiritual gifts (1 Corinthians 12:12, 20).

How then, should we answer the question, "Why do we need the Church?" Our answer in this space will be shaped to address we who are in the Church. Many who don't believe in Christ see no need for the Church, thinking that we read and worship a version of a Mother Goose fairy tale. They are entitled to their belief system—that is what it is. On this side of belief there are those who feel that since the church is filled with hypocrites, they can worship and engage in self-study and avoid drama by maintaining their membership at the Greater Bedside Baptist Tabernacle. The reality is that the Church has always lived with not being a perfect body. In 1 Corinthians, Paul chastises a man who has slept with his stepmother (5:1), takes issue with believers taking one another to court (6:1-11), and calls out members who got drunk during the Lord's Supper (11:21).

The other side of this coin is that when we operate as a solo Christian bereft of the body of Christ, we set ourselves up to be against a portion of ourselves, which is the very body that is a part of Christ Himself. In plain language, we cut off our nose to spite our face. The truth is that all of us are flawed, and as last Sunday's sermon (anchored in Matthew 7:5) taught us, we need to remove the plank from our own eyes. We are reminded through this that one of the major functions of the Church is to be a "hospital for sinners," and we all qualify. Through the local church, we help each other grow into deeper spiritual development, for we are to care for one another because we all triumph or suffer together (1 Corinthians 12: 25-26). We also go out into the world spreading the Gospel and doing the work of missions both at home and abroad (Matthew 28:18-20; Acts 1:8).

So, each of us belong to the universal Church, and each of us, as Christians, should be active in a local church. We commonly refer to it as "being a church member." Being a church member means sharing fully in the life of your church. Every church member should attend worship regularly; witness and share God's love in their lives; serve God and their neighbor responsibly and faithfully; and give of their time, talent and money to further the church's mission locally and throughout the world. When we do this, the Church grows and so do we. One thing is clear—God designed the Church for all of us to take part in the great work of God's Kingdom on Earth. It is a privilege for God to call on flawed humans to be a major part of executing this heavenly mission.

Necessary Nuggets about the Church: Church Finances and How They Work July 6, 2014

Today we visit our second installment of "Necessary Nuggets about the Church." Our subject in this entry is church finances and how they work. The reality of the church is that money should follow ministry. In other words, the plans of the church should be supported with resources; resources should never be gathered merely for the sake of hoarding.

In a typical church, you will see several basic accounts—the Current Expense Fund, the Building Fund, the account for Clubs and Auxiliaries, and Resources (savings) if they exist. These are the general names for these accounts that you will find in many churches. The Current Expense Fund operates for a church like the household checking account, for it handles all of the common expenses for the church. It is the account where the church pays for general and ministry expenses. Payroll, evangelism, and outreach all get their money from the Current Expense Fund, for it is the basic financial lifeblood of the church. Many churches don't have any savings to speak of, and may not have any other financial instruments, but *every* church has a Current Expense Fund (a checking account). And when money is raised for pet projects without supporting the Current Expense Fund, the church cannot fulfill its ministry obligations and it suffers. This goes for present and any future ministry thrusts. If the Current Expense Fund is kept anemic, the church suffers. Look at it this way- if your personal checking account has problems, *you* have problems.

In most churches the Building Fund isn't used to put up a building. It is the Capital Improvement Fund. If something needs to be added to the church, or purchased that will help the physical structure and/or work of the church, this fund is used. Need an organ? A copier? A handicap accessible ramp? This is the place. The Clubs and Auxiliaries account is where monies for the various church groups are kept (instead of in someone's home). Resources for future use are collected in special accounts for a specific purpose; it could be anything from a building to a new ministry initiative.

The important thing to remember is to support your church through your giving. The proper giving in a very basic way is through the Current Expense Fund. When you focus on a pet project and ignore the Current Expense Fund you weaken the church. Said another way, if you fully fund your pet project, and don't support the Current Expense Fund, will the church continue to exist?

Next week, we will look at some specific areas of ministry in the church. As you look at this today, know that without tangible support, ministry is hampered, and all of the things you want to see in your church can't, won't, and don't happen.

Necessary Nuggets about the Church: The "Business" of the Church
July 13, 2014

Go therefore and make disciples of all nations, baptizing them in the name of the Father and of the Son and of the Holy Spirit, and teaching them to obey everything that I have commanded you. And remember, I am with you always, to the end of the age (Matthew 28:19-20 NRSV).

But you will receive power when the Holy Spirit has come upon you; and you will be my witnesses in Jerusalem, in all Judea and Samaria, and to the ends of the earth (Acts 1:8 ESV).

Therefore, if anyone is in Christ, he is a new creation; the old has gone, the new has come (2 Corinthians 5:17)!

We are now in our third installment of "Necessary Nuggets about the Church." Today's focus will be on the 'business" of the Church; in other words, what does the Church do that makes it both unique and necessary in the world?

The Church is designed to accomplish life transformation from the inside out. Through a relationship with Jesus Christ, we change and grow. This is the purpose of being a part of the "body" of Christ; for although we use organizational principles, we are an *organism*. Understanding this definition reminds us that an organism *must grow*, or die.

Since the church is designed for growth, how does this happen? We do it in several ways that are very basic. We must understand that the marketing methods and branding plans we employ in the 21st century merely jumpstart the basics already put in place by the Lord. If the basics aren't in place, the Church merely mirrors someone with an infection; there is unhealthy swelling but no growth. Missions—the act of actively using both works of help and witness—is the basic bedrock of the Church. As the Acts passage found above states, this should take place locally and abroad. The reference to going to Samaria is code language for engaging in mission work with people you dislike and/or who are not like you.

Coupled with missions is evangelism and discipleship. Evangelism is the spreading of the news of the Gospel. It is one thirsty person telling others about the great oasis he or she has found. Discipleship is the completion of the evangelistic process so that the one who has found Jesus can go out and effectively witness His teachings to others. So often we stop at evangelism, if we do it at all, and forget discipleship. Many in the church today are not disciples; for disciples, as we see in the Matthew text, would learn and do everything taught to them and have the ability to teach it to others.

Everything that we've said so far comes together when we talk about the life transformation business. Want the church to be more visible? Want to see more programs centered on outreach? Engage in life transformation. Support the work of the church through tithes and offerings. Want to see change? It won't happen in a healthy, sustainable way without being obedient in executing the business of life transformation.

The neighborhoods around our churches are ripe for the Gospel. The neighborhoods in which we live are the same. Every day as we watch the news, television shows, movies, and talk to everyday people, it is obvious that the world needs a genuine encounter with Jesus through those who have had one themselves. This is where the life transformative power of our business will make a substantial difference. In knowing this, we can begin to be the salt of the earth that Jesus intended for us to be.

Maybe we have concentrated too much on churches maintaining their position, instead of conquering with the Gospel. After all, transformation isn't a passive activity.

CHAPTER SIX - MORE REFLECTIONS ON THE CHRISTIAN LIFE AND YOU

Whom Should We Emulate—Judas or Jesus?
March 19, 2017

In the op-ed piece by Nicholas Kristof in last Thursday's *New York Times*, we read the following words:

A woman who had been bleeding for 12 years came up behind Jesus and touched his clothes in hope of a cure. Jesus turned to her and said: "Fear not. Because of your faith, you are now healed."
Then spoke Pious Paul of Ryan: "But teacher, is that wise? When you cure her, she learns dependency. Then the poor won't take care of themselves, knowing that you'll always bail them out! You must teach them personal responsibility!"
They were interrupted by 10 lepers who stood at a distance and shouted, "Jesus, have pity on us."
"NO!" shouted Pious Paul. "Jesus! You don't have time. We have a cocktail party fund-raiser in the temple. And don't worry about them — they've already got health care access."[xxxv]

America, in my opinion, will now begin to see that we've begun the era of two deceptive bookends—smoke and mirrors, and three-card monte. In his piece, Kristof alludes to the CBO (Congressional Budget Office), a bipartisan committee that has shown the error of embracing the proposed healthcare proposals being pushed in Washington. Its cost per individual would be catastrophic for the average American. Looking at the other bookend, President Trump in his first proposed budget will increase defense and homeland security spending; this includes over $1 billion for the infrastructure around the border wall. Meanwhile, this proposal would also eliminate funding for nearly 20 smaller independent agencies, including the National Endowment for the Arts, the National Endowment for the Humanities, the Corporation for Public Broadcasting and the Legal Services Corporation. The bottom line is this budget would signal a radical shift in much of the nation. Like the deceptive trickery of a three-card monte game, the only winner would be the rich while the persons who voted for and supported Trump lose. We would also suffer.

What I share today goes beyond partisan politics or personal preference. It speaks to priorities and a world view in a society seemingly post literate, where history is what happened last month and reading is optional. Because of this, we now live during a time of "alternative facts." Here, for me, is the real issue:

> *Six days before the Passover, Jesus arrived at Bethany, where Lazarus lived, whom Jesus had raised from the dead. Here a dinner was given in Jesus' honor. Martha served, while Lazarus was among those reclining at the table with him. Then Mary took about a pint of pure nard, an expensive perfume; she poured it on Jesus' feet and wiped his feet with her hair. And the house was filled with the fragrance of the perfume.*
>
> *But one of his disciples, Judas Iscariot, who was later to betray him, objected, "Why wasn't this perfume sold and the money given to the poor? It was worth a year's wages" He did not say this because he cared about the poor but because he was a thief; as keeper of the money bag, he used to help himself to what was put into it.*
>
> *"Leave her alone," Jesus replied. "It was intended that she should save this perfume for the day of my burial. You will al-*

> *ways have the poor among you, but you will not always have me (John 12:1-8)."*

Whom should we emulate—Judas or Jesus?

What is the "Business" of the Church? September 10, 2000

I am of the opinion that we live during a time when the American Church is unclear about its mission. In short, we don't seem to understand what "business" we are in. Some of our churches act as if we are in the entertainment business. They take on all of the attributes of worldly venues to get people to unite with their local church. Some of our churches act as if we are museums. It is their feeling that we should preserve all things that we have done in the past, regardless of whether they are applicable to the present and the future. Many local congregations feel they are in competition with other local assemblies, forgetting that we are part of the Church Universal and therefore on the same team. All of these perspectives miss the point, and if we're honest, we can see some of our personal preferences in all of them.

If we give serious thought to the church's business, it should be obvious. The Church only has *one* business. It is a business that will exist as long as people do. It is not contingent on weather conditions or the stock market. Politicians, principalities and powers cannot stop it; in fact, their persecution tends to help increase business. The overall sickness of humanity fuels the need for the church, and ensures its relevance in society, provided it remembers the nature of its "business."

The Church is in the life transformation business. Stating this in a concise, succinct manner may make this concept hard to understand. However, think about it. When Jesus Christ comes into a life, He *transforms* that life. The Bible, in

2 Corinthians 5:17 says, *therefore, if anyone is in Christ, he is a new creation; the old has gone, the new has come!* After Jesus enters your life, transformation continues. This is known as the pursuit of holiness, or sanctification. It is the act of living the Christian life. Our foreparents described it this way: "Every day with Jesus is sweeter than the day before."

In light of this reality, we must realize that everything we do as a church should point to life transformation. If it doesn't, it is taking us away from our business focus, and causing us to lose relevance in the world. It will be, as Jesus said, a matter of the salt losing *its savor* (Matthew 5:13 KJV), becoming useful only as sawdust for wiping dirty feet.

The Place of Healing and Forgiveness
July 22, 2001

We live in a time where the need for personal and systemic healing is great. People are broken, wounded and hurting. Some are confused, alienated and alone. There are major societal disconnects in the family structure, and in many causes and institutions that once gave power and security to the human landscape. With all of the self-help books and seminars available on the market today, you would think that we could finally put our brokenness to rest. However, it is obvious that something else, some other mechanism must exist to make possible our personal and societal healing.

Personal healing ultimately takes place through Jesus Christ. When we have a relationship with Jesus Christ, we have positioned ourselves so that healing can begin. The other step in the healing process is one that for many is unpopular. Jesus explains it this way:

Matthew 5:23-24: "*Therefore, if you are offering your gift at the altar and there remember that your brother has something against you, leave your gift there in front of the altar. First go and be reconciled to your brother; then come and offer your gift.*

Matthew 5:43-47: *You have heard that it was said, `Love your neighbor and hate your enemy.' But I tell you: Love your enemies and pray for those who persecute you, that you may be sons of your Father in heaven. He causes his sun to rise on the evil and the good, and sends rain on the righteous and the unrighteous. If you love those who love you, what reward will you get? Are not even the tax collectors* *doing that? And if you greet only your brothers, what are you doing more than others? Do not even pagans do that?*

Matthew 18:21, 22: *Then Peter came to Jesus and asked, "Lord, how many times shall I forgive my brother when he sins against me? Up to seven times?" Jesus answered, "I tell you, not seven times, but seventy-seven times.*

Forgiveness allows healing for the one who is injured. It gives such a one the ability to move forward with life. So often, those who bear grudges get sick, die, or wear out long before the one guilty of the crime. The act of forgiveness also makes room for reconciliation.

Finally, there are two things to consider when one views forgiveness. First, all of us, before our relationship with Jesus Christ, were guilty of doing wrong against God. And yet, through Jesus Christ we have been forgiven and restored. On this side of Jordan, God allows each of us the chance to be forgiven. This is why we are to forgive, so that we can live in the example set by Christ and allow some of our transgressors an opportunity for God's grace. Second, the ability to forgive is a sign that the forgiver knows God. This is greater than any platitude one can receive. Let us all imitate Christ as we look to forgive those who have wronged us, committing their change to God.

An Internal Preparation
August 5, 2001

As we arrive at this the first Sunday of August, many of us realize that school is right around the corner. The county school system begins classes next week, and the Memphis system the following week. In addition, many of our college students are making final preparations for their departure for school and the next semester. Many adults have taken the last days of a final vacation fling before the depths of winter take hold.

In the midst of this preparation, have we taken the time to spiritually prepare our children? Columbine and Paducah, Pearl and Baltimore, in addition to thousands of episodes across this nation should tell us and remind us of the societal dysfunction taking place in our schools. Teaching was once a most attractive profession in our community; now the talk surrounding a lot of teaching is anchored around the need for combat pay. With the specter of violence in schools, this notion has shifted from a joke in bad taste to a reality found in many places. We have searched for the answer, but the solution is often one of the spirit. In Matthew 15, the scribes and Pharisees challenged Jesus. They could not understand how a knowledgeable teacher like Jesus would not be concerned about keeping one's hands ceremonially clean while eating. Jesus responded by saying, *...what goes into a man's mouth does not make him `unclean,' but what comes out of his mouth, that is what makes him `unclean...don't you see that whatever enters the mouth goes into the stomach and then out of the body? But the things that come out of the mouth come from the heart, and these make a man `unclean.' For out of the heart come evil thoughts, murder, adultery,* *sexual immorality, theft, false testimony, slander. These are what make a man `unclean;' but eating with unwashed hands does not make him `unclean'* (Matthew 15:11, 17-25).

We spend an inordinate amount of time addressing the external. Grooming, for example, seems to take precedence over praying. We will chide our youth for untucked shirt tails, but do we encourage them to pray? In the spirit of placing proper focus on interior realities, we will have special prayer for our youth during today's worship. We will pray for their educational success and focus, their safety, their Christian witness, and their ability to make the right choices. I realize that many of us do this on a private level, but there is power in doing this on a corporate one. Remember the strength that you perhaps received from hearing a parent or grandparent pray on your behalf. Our children, residents of the 21st century, need and deserve the same experience on a corporate level.

The Exterior and the Interior
June 30, 2002

As of this writing, the renovation of our sanctuary is underway. At the completion of the work, our sanctuary should have an updated look and increased functionality. While this is going on, many of you have probably noticed and used our new phone system. In addition to our current renovation project, we've updated several areas in our church building over the past few years. All of these improvements are designed to help sharpen our efficiency as the "greatest church in the created order."

Also, today we celebrate the installment of a historical marker on our church grounds, culminating the placement of our church building on the National Register of Historic Places, which took place on July 14, 2000. First Baptist is now a part of the Historical Markers Program, begun in the 1950's to mark the locations of sites, events, and people significant in Tennessee history. A very casual and slight look at our history as a church will note the important role our church has played in the history of our state.

Renovation. Recognition. History. Innovation. The future. All of these areas are important, yet there is another that must be considered and addressed. In some ways, we have taken a man, suited him up and recognized his past. Let us, for discussion's sake, say that this man is Muhammad Ali. Ali is about 60 years young; he looks good for his age. He is the former heavyweight champion of the world, and within him still burns the fire of a great boxer. But, would you send him back into the ring to fight anyone? While his interior life may be as vibrant as it was years ago, the exterior physical life of Ali—his age and his Parkinson's disease—makes this prohibitive.

We must look at our interior life as a corporate witness in order to perpetuate and access the achievements that have brought us to this day. We must recognize that the accolades of this day will be given because *the people who made up First Baptist in its past made a difference.* God's Church is made up of people. God's Church, as individual congregations, takes up residence in buildings, from which the mission of the Church reaches into the community. These individual congregations meet God in worship in the sanctuary, which is the place in the building set aside for the specific worship and presence of God. God, not each other, is the audience of our worship, and all that we do in worship should be directed toward God. The sanctuary is important because after a week of challenges and strife, it is the place where we gather to meet God, and the place where God has promised to meet us.

Today, as we look at the historical marker and the renovated sanctuary, let us as individuals rededicate our lives to God. The exterior has worth, but through wear and tear can and will wear away. Our strength, both individually and collectively, is found in our interior connection to the Lord. We often work on our exterior; our hair, clothes and accoutrements. What really matters, however, is what is on the inside. If we place our focus on God, we will begin to rededicate and reenergize ourselves to serving God through God's vehicle of engaging the world, the church.

Then we will add new chapters to an already great legacy of faith.

The Necessity of Your Church
July 14, 2002

Your church is the most important entity in your community. Not the school, although it is a place of learning. Not places of commerce and manufacturing, although they provide jobs. Not places attached to the medical field, although they help improve our quality of life. The government and the vast cadre of people trying to become part of the government will try to make you think that your survival depends on them. They may have some importance, but they pale in comparison to your church. They see the importance of the Church in a clearer way, sometimes, than its members; come election time they send letters and make their presence known in local places of worship. All during the week, salesmen, both Christian and non-Christian, try to unload the latest bells and whistles onto the Church. Satan or his cohorts, known as demons, will even show up from time to time; the Bible records in Job how Satan would show up in heaven when the angels gathered before God. You may not see it or appreciate it, but your church is the most important entity in your life.

In order to understand the importance of the Church to you, the question must be asked, "What does the Church do for me?" First, church gives you a moral foundation. Everyone needs a compass for the vast wilderness we know as life. Without it, we wander without purpose or chase after the wrong things. The "golden rule," originating in Luke 6:31, *Do [un]to others as you would have them do [un]to you*, is powerful. Think of what the world would be like if more people would commit to this simple truth! These wise words from Jesus would not make sense without the moral foundation that your church gives you. This foundation comes from God. We have recently seen the tragedy of having no moral absolutes. For example, Wall Street is rocking and reeling from the misdeeds of various sectors of corporate America. This issue has even reached the halls of government, as Vice President Cheney has been named as part of a lawsuit. Obedience to the simple moral absolute taught in church—*Thou shalt not steal* (Exodus 20:15)—would have prevented our economic roller coaster ride. Every CEO, every accountant, every politician comes from a community that contains a church from which they can receive a moral foundation. This is the value of your church.

Second, church is a place where you gain strength to continue to live in the world. Because of Adam and Eve, we live by the sweat of our brow with pain, sorrow and death intertwined into our existence. Your church is a place where you learn how to live in the midst of a sin sick world, utilizing the power of God to overcome all obstacles.

Third, church is where you connect your earthly existence to an eternal reality. All of us reside on Earth with an extended visa. This world is not our permanent home. Our life span is but one grain of sand on the beach of eternity. That eternity can be blissful or painful—it's our choice. The Church offers us a relationship with Jesus Christ, who has promised to send us a Comforter (the Holy Spirit) on Earth and prepare a home for us in heaven. We are the messengers of this good news. This news has transformed lives and communities, and with all the challenges that we face individually and collectively, this is the only news that can bring permanent change. Your church is the most important entity in your community.

Comforting Promises of God
September 8, 2002

As we gather this Sunday, several issues swirl around us as a collective body. Over the past few weeks, our church secretary and several of our members have become ill, some suddenly. This coming Wednesday will be the first anniversary of the Pearl Harbor for this generation, as we remember how our country was violated by terrorists. Locally, between an increase in home invasions and the general spate of bad news, it appears that we might be safer in dealing with unknown distant dangers than the unlawful among our own neighbors.

When we consider the events in our congregation, city, and nation, we become aware of the suddenness of it all. We make plans; circumstances change them. We assume the course of a day at its beginning, then like a flooded, raging river, the day suddenly shifts. Where does God stand during these times? Here are some of God's promises:

Hebrews 13:5: *Keep your lives free from the love of money and be content with what you have, because God has said, "Never will I leave you; never will I forsake you."*

Matthew 28:20: *…and teaching them to obey everything I have commanded you. And surely I am with you always, to the very end of the age."*

John 14:16: *And I will pray the Father, and he shall give you another Comforter, that he may abide with you forever;* (KJV)

Psalm 37:25: *I was young and now I am old, yet I have never seen the righteous forsaken or their children begging bread.*

Psalm 46:1-7: *God [is] our refuge and strength, a very present help in trouble. Therefore will not we fear, though the earth be removed, and though the mountains be carried into the midst of the sea; [Though] the waters thereof roar [and] be troubled, [though] the mountains shake with the swelling thereof. [There is] a river, the streams whereof shall make glad the city of God, the holy [place] of the tabernacles of the most High. God [is] in the midst of her; she shall not be moved: God shall help her, [and that] right early. The heathen raged, the kingdoms were moved: he uttered his voice, the earth melted. The LORD of hosts [is] with us; the God of Jacob [is] our refuge* (KJV).

God never promises that trouble and challenge will be nonexistent. We are promised God's presence, and the awareness that we will never be separated from God's presence, power and protection. In stormy times, we find ourselves willing students in God's classroom as we learn more about Him. I pray that during this week you will listen for what God is saying as we try to understand all of the things happening around us.

What Does Your Checkbook Register Say About You?
April 6, 2003

When was the last time you looked at your checkbook register? I realize that every time you write a check you see it, but do you really observe its inflow and outflow? Maybe you never considered it, but your checkbook tells the day-to-day story of your life. It shows how much you earn, and how often you receive a paycheck. It reveals your bills—their quantity and their individual sizes. Your hobbies and interests are also reflected, for very few people carry cash in large quantities. If you are one who uses a credit card for many purchases, your register will show how much of your disposable income is used for your leisure. It also shows times of emergency and unexpected expenses. Your checkbook register tells your story better and louder than you could ever do verbally.

Your checkbook register also testifies how you feel about God. The Bible often speaks about money. Here is one passage where Scripture states its position:

Matthew 6:19-24: *Do not store up for yourselves treasures on earth, where moth and rust destroy, and where thieves break in and steal. But store up for yourselves treasures in heaven, where moth and rust do not destroy, and where thieves do not break in and steal. For where your treasure is, there your heart will be also. "The eye is the lamp of the body. If your eyes are good, your whole body will be full of light. But if your eyes are bad, your whole body will be full of darkness. If then the light within you is darkness, how great is that darkness! "No one can serve two masters. Either he will hate the one* *and love the other, or he will be devoted to the one and despise the other. You cannot serve both God and Money.*

The above words of Jesus should cause us to take a look at our priorities. Many of us pay our bills, spend on our hobbies and interests, and give God what is left over. Often this is not much. God asks for tithes and offerings, and many times we render a tip. For example, it is common in churches for many to give $20 a month. The median household income in Shelby County is $39,593. A tithing family receiving this income would contribute about $3,960 a year; this would be $330 *a month.* The $20 a month giver would contribute $240 *a year* to the Lord's cause. It has been documented in several places that churchgoers earn more per capita than non-churchgoers, and people with postgraduate or professional degrees earn more than those with a bachelor's. The point is simple—I pray that God never blesses us in the same way that we tip Him. God provides intellect, opportunity and income. Every deposit and withdrawal entered in our checkbook registry is possible because of God's goodness. It is time for us to show our appreciation to God from the very place we parade our actual lifestyle the loudest—from our checkbook.

How Should We View Bad Luck?
October 19, 2003

This week the Chicago Cubs were on the brink of making their first entrance into the World Series since 1945. Wednesday night they saw their immediate chance fly south to the city of Miami. What makes this a story worthy of note is the "curse of the billy goat." During the 1945 World Series a bar owner wanted to enter the Cubs ballpark with a goat. He even bought a ticket for it! Chicago was cosmopolitan even then, and the goat, after making it into the ballpark, was rightfully ejected with its owner. The goat's owner then placed a curse on the Cubs, similar to the so-called curse on Ham (Ham was never cursed—see Genesis 9), where he pronounced that the Cubs would never play a World Series game in Wrigley Field again. Over the years fans have tried to reverse the curse; but almost 60 years later, this curse has held firm.

Many pundits will continue to attribute the Cubs' loss to the curse or bad luck. Some might even blame it on God. This curse raises some questions that call out for an answer. I bring these things to our attention realizing that on many levels sports is merely entertainment. On the other hand, I would encourage you not to attempt telling the diehard sports fan that life and death aren't in each game. People have been injured and lives have been lost throughout the world based on the outcome of a sporting match.

Realizing this, let's look at this "curse." First, to believe this curse assumes that the goat owner had the power to enforce it. It is said that this gentleman died over 30 years ago. Even when he lived, he had no real power over the Cubs' destiny. Second, in this age of so-called sophistication, when to believe in God and moral absolutes is considered foolish, it's ironic that grown men would even give credence to a goat and his owner. Third, it points to how we view God. Many think that God has limited power, and we only use God when it is convenient for our desired outcome. For example, if both the Marlins and Cubs have Christians on their roster and fan base, does God, who is no respecter of persons, love the Marlins more since they beat the Cubs? Believe it or not, some people reserve their prayer life for their favorite team or when they are neck deep in trouble.

The billy goat curse shows us on some level that people want to believe in something to give explanation and meaning to the ebb and flow of life. Scripture tells us in Romans chapter 1 that the evidence of God's power and divine nature are clearly seen, and reminds us in Psalms 14:1 that only a fool would say there is no God. Every person in some way wants to ultimately find God. We also see this reaffirmed in the Great Commission given to us by Jesus. If we would but prayerfully go out into the larger world, we could bring with us the answer for life found in Jesus Christ. Otherwise, those who don't know the Lord will continue to tie their future to a "curse."

The One with True Vision
November 9, 2003

Human beings have been gifted with limited vision. God has anchored us in time, and we must walk by time's schedule to move from the past in making the future the present. Paul says it this way: ...*now we see but a poor reflection as in a mirror* (1 Corinthians 13:12). We cannot see from the inside of our homes what is happening outside unless we are looking through a window; we cannot see from the outside what is happening indoors except by the same means.

Because we have limited vision, things that seem bleak are sometimes the beginning of blessings. Human sinfulness led to the slave trade, which seemed to have no end. But God moved on the hearts of several, and beginning in 1808 and ending in 1888, slavery was abolished throughout the world. Jim Crow became entrenched in our land, and now it is a shadow of what it was. The Civil Rights Movement was the vehicle of change. Since the 1960's, we have seen the dismantling of two godless systems of government; communism and apartheid. For many of us, these developments were in the realm of the impossible; but with God, all things are possible.

In the Old Testament, there was a servant of Elisha who didn't understand the problem of limited vision. One morning he stuck his head outside of their tent and saw the Aramean army. He ran to Elisha and asked, "Oh, my lord, what shall we do?" Elisha told him, "Don't be afraid...those who are with us are more than those who are with them." Elisha then prayed, "O LORD, open his eyes so he may see." The Bible then says *the LORD opened the servant's eyes, and he looked and saw the hills full of horses and chariots of fire all around Elisha* (2 Kings 6:17-18). Elisha then asked God to strike the Arameans with blindness, and afterwards lead them to the king of Israel where they were fed and sent home. Because of this, the warfare and raiding from the nation of Aram ceased. All of this took place because Elisha did not rely on his limited vision but accessed spiritual vision.

Challenges are always present, whether they are in our church family, jobs, or personal life. Yet, God continues to be present and asks of us to utilize spiritual vision that comes from a relationship with Him to see His hand in the midst of circumstances. Some things come into our lives as a test, others as a wake-up call, and yet others as a result of our faith. But in everything, God has promised never to leave us or forsake us, for as Jesus has said, *lo, I am with you always, [even] unto the end of the world* (Matthew 28:20 KJV).

How Do You View Your Religion?
March 7, 2004

We find ourselves in the third month of a year that has been quite interesting. A president once secure in the polls appears to be close to losing his job. The definition of marriage receives challenges. And a movie about Jesus, which usually would be ignored by all but a few is now setting box office records. In all of these scenarios, religion is a part of the conversation.

Some view religion as a bad thing. It divides rather than unites, some say. Yet, without a moral compass we as humans tend to sink into free-fall. The headlines even this week bear witness to this. When you read the texts of the world's major religions, all speak to tolerance of each other and the ability to treat one's neighbor as oneself. People who are truly religious are an asset, not a detriment, to society.

This brings to mind an important issue. Built into each of us is a desire to connect with the Divine. If unrecognized or unnurtured, it can become a search that leads to doing the wrong things in the wrong places. Do you then make this search into a vehicle created and shaped by men, or do you attempt to connect to God through a move on God's part?

During this season of Lent we move toward that Friday when the One who was fully God and fully man endured horrible brutality at the hands of men. This was done because of His love for us. Therefore, being a Christian is not just a process of involving oneself in a religious system, but it is a personal relationship with God undergirded by love. This love caused God Himself to die on a cross for the sins of the world.

Through His work accomplished on Calvary, Jesus leaves us to spread the good news of His love. God now gives us opportunities through current events to show the world the preached sermon of our lives. If we would but do this, the invitation to discipleship will yield much fruit.

How Should You Handle Your Anger?
June 18, 2017

"In your anger do not sin": Do not let the sun go down while you are still angry (Ephesians 4:26).

An angry man stirs up dissension, and a hot-tempered one commits many sins (Proverbs 29:22).

Anger – a pervasive emotion in our society. It is an emotion that has no negative value in its own right. When used properly, it can cause a community to create a bus boycott, and make a woman named Fannie Lou Hamer say, "I'm sick and tired of being sick and tired." However, without the proper use and perspective, it can be an uncontrollable bomb that eradicates both the angry and those in close proximity.

This past week, a two-year-old died here in Memphis after being a passenger in a car targeted by senseless road rage. In Arlington, Virginia, a Bernie Sanders supporter, unhappy with the current direction of our national government, decided to take inappropriate action while heavily laced with calculated rage. He approached a softball practice where Republican lawmakers from the House of Representatives were on the field, and after confirming this fact, went on a shooting spree. His self-defined mission seemingly was to kill the opposition.

Malcolm X, if he were here, would clear his throat and remind us that we created this monster. That's the meaning of his quote, "The chickens have come home to roost." We have bathed our reality in violence since the birth of our nation, and now our means of common discourse is a lack of civility because to govern our temper is considered weak. Conflict resolution, and the use of anger constructively is now about as commonplace as a two-dollar bill.

Appropriate gun control laws, destruction of systemic ills that created the current hot-bed climate, and non-violent resolution of disagreements should be the everyday plan. But, before the legislative pieces of this equation can be complete, there is a role for us to play.

How many times have you addressed someone in anger? Called them out of their name? Killed their reputation because at the time you were upset? Encouraged someone to act with their emotions instead of their mind? Maybe the scenario ended differently, but it's in the same vein as our two examples that ended in tragedy. If we consider the two portions of Scripture cited above, we and many others can avoid the tragedies that happen when anger rules the day.

CHAPTER SEVEN - THE CHRISTIAN LIFE AND YOU, 3 TIMES THE CHARM

Instead of Looking Busy, Be Busy
March 30, 2008

This past week, I had the pleasure of being in a city-wide gathering where the master of ceremonies told an interesting joke. He told of driving by a building laced with graffiti, and the most visible and notable writing proclaimed, "Jesus is coming soon—look busy." Needless to say, this particular joke caught my attention.

As I left the gathering, I began to think about the message behind this joke. Too often, as flawed human beings, our focus is on looking busy. We involve ourselves in work that seems important, but in the final analysis is merely designed to give us something to do. Matthew 25 relates to us the story of the ten virgins—five were wise and five were foolish. All ten were waiting for the arrival of the bridegroom, but only the five wise virgins came prepared to work. The five foolish virgins merely wanted to look busy, but when they saw that work was necessary, they hurriedly tried to make up for lost time. But it was too late. We are encouraged in Matthew 25:13 to ...*keep watch, because you do not know the day or the hour.*

Our compassion for others, and our commitment to Christ, is the work which is everlasting and God-pleasing. "Looking busy" is part of the focus of today's sermon. Often, as Paul says, we have the form of godliness but lack its power. This happens because running in place is easier than running the race. However, the world is counting on us to provide leadership, and point the way to God. Those in the world are looking for God but are searching in the wrong places. We must do our job, not merely look busy. Remember, we each had someone in our lives who was vigilant, and we came to know Christ. This is best summed up by the words of the great hymn, "Only What You Do for Christ Will Last", by Raymond Rasberry:

You may build great cathedrals large or small,
You can build skyscrapers grand and tall,
You may conquer all the failures of the past,
But only what you do for Christ will last.
Remember only what you do for Christ will last;
...Only what you do for Him will be counted at the end,
Only what you do for Christ will last. [xxxvi]

Proper Vision
June 28, 2009

1 Samuel 16:6-7: *When they came, he looked on Elias and thought, "Surely the LORD's anointed is now before the LORD." But the LORD said to Samuel, "Do not look on his appearance or on the height of his stature, because I have rejected him; for the LORD does not see as mortals see; they look on the outward appearance, but the LORD looks on the heart."* (NRSV)

Among optometrists, 20/20 vision for mortals is the beginning of an acceptable range of natural sight. It allows you or me to go through daily tasks without the need for eyeglasses or contact lenses. This condition also assumes that we have proper vision, for the designation of 20/20 sight affirms that we can easily see all that we should see, unaided and unassisted. But can we?

In a *Time* magazine article, "Is an Ugly Baby Harder to Love?", a new study states that the better looking a baby is when born, the more a mother loves him or her. Other studies in other places clearly document that beautiful people get better treatment than those considered average looking. Interesting indeed!

Our text is part of the larger story of when the prophet Samuel anoints David as the king of Israel. Samuel is clearly listening to God for instruction on whom to anoint, and has Jesse, the patriarch of the house, parade his sons before him. In our text Samuel, for a brief moment, relies only on his 20/20 natural vision, and the Lord corrects him, indicating that there is more than what the physical eye can see.

How many times have you allowed yourself to be smitten by a beautiful person of the opposite sex, only to find out that this was the worst decision of your life? Have you ever done business with someone because they had perfect diction, perfect conversation, and perfect haberdashery only to be swindled out of some good money? How many times have you settled for shoddy business, been disrespected in relationships, abused emotionally, and taken advantage of time and time again because the appearance of the individual(s) did something—in your mind—to increase your stature and standing among those around you? Would you admit that when the smoke cleared, when the luster wore off, you were holding a big bag of unfulfilled empty fantasies?

All of us need proper vision. This is seeing the world, and those in it, the way God does. This means dealing with people based on their interior life, and not the exterior package that they may have through no fault or good fortune of their own. It also means having a heart shaped around love and service of the Lord, which will then be seen by others. A person who solely lives by exterior sight gives little attention to the shaping of what is important, and is tossed to and fro by what they see. When you walk by sight, you limit yourself to only what you see, which is constantly changing. As people of faith anchored in Jesus Christ, we already know how we should maintain proper vision; walking by FAITH, and not by sight. So…how are you going to view and treat those you meet and speak to from now on?

The Façade of Civility
September 27, 2009

Matthew 15:10-11: *Then he called the crowd to him and said to them, "Listen and understand: it is not what goes into the mouth that defiles a person, but it is what comes out of the mouth that defiles"* (NRSV).

Three incidents in the recent past have caused some to question out loud whether communal civility has expired. A tennis star inappropriately yells at a line judge during play, which ultimately costs her the match, followed about a day later by a famous rapper interrupting a presentation during an awards show to give his opinion. Finally, Congressman Joe Wilson of South Carolina did the unthinkable in yelling out, "You lie!" during President Obama's speech to a joint session of Congress. This has never happened in the history of our country.

Where has civility gone? Oh, you mean the civility of chains, nooses, inappropriately used fire engine hoses, beatings, and threats? It's become a part of history. You must mean the *façade* of civility. We do a great job in our society of covering up who we really are, and showing off our acting skills to the world. Some folks would rather have people who can't stand them speak to them like long lost friends instead of being true to their feelings. The façade of civility is expected and encouraged, and those that breach it find themselves viewed as people of low breeding. The problem with this view is that it ignores the definition of a façade, which in simple language is a pretense. It is like a Hollywood movie set—a make believe world. This is what Jesus was alluding to in the above text.

In Matthew 15, beginning with verse 1, Jesus was asked the question, *Why do your disciples break the tradition of the elders? For they do not wash their hands before they eat* (ESV). The key phrase is, "break the tradition of the elders." Those asking weren't concerned with cleanliness, but appearance. For them, observing the tradition was the façade of civility. Notice Jesus' answer—He basically asks them why they don't live what they profess, for their lips say one thing but their hearts are far from God.

Our text cited above merely says that the way a person is will eventually reveal itself. Serena Williams was extremely angry about a blown call, Kanye West has had issues seemingly since his mother's death, besides believing his own press releases, and Joe Wilson—who is said to have held leadership positions in the Sons of Confederate Veterans—may have just had a flashback moment when looking in the face of a Black president. The ultimate issue, then, isn't civility. That is a facade, or even more direct, a mirage. The real issue is the need for life transformation. This is what Jesus gives.

Who Should be Our Role Model?
December 13, 2009

1 **Corinthians 11:1:** *Be imitators of me, as I am of Christ* (NRSV).

Over the past week, we have heard much concerning Tiger Woods and his infidelities. Many have a running tab, keeping track of the latest person willingly and quickly jumping into the spotlight to tell of her part in Mr. Woods' unfaithfulness. His name is added to a long list of athletes, entertainers, and yes, Christians, who have been caught in wrong doing.

When these things come out, we have varied reactions. Some look down on all members of the opposite sex. Others, if the perpetrator is a Christian—especially a clergyperson—see it as proof of the false nature, they believe, of the Church. What we should realize is we now live in a culture where we are well practiced in building up our heroes in preparation to tear them down. We seek in them the perfection that we will never possess; for we reason that if they can hit a ball, sing a song, or use mellifluous language better than us then they live minus any flaws.

This posture will not work, for discarding heroes at the slightest sign of indiscretion or imperfection is like chopping down trees for firewood—it must be a continuous activity, and it eventually produces barren land. Perhaps we need to find an alternative way of viewing each other. I submit that this way already exists, and we can find it in the New Testament. The apostle Paul says in 1 Corinthians

11:1, *Be imitators of me, as I am of Christ.* Paul, well known and well respected, was telling the church he organized, "Look past me to the Jesus in me. Wherever I fall short, look at Jesus instead." The Bible reminds us in Isaiah 64:6 that, *all our righteousnesses are as filthy rags* (KJV). If you understood what that actually means in its original language—Hebrew—you would know that God has a low view of our perceived perfection, because it doesn't exist. So, if none of us are righteous, then ultimately there is a higher standard, a greater level of perfection that we should imitate beyond ourselves.

I believe that God allowed some of the above controversy during this Christmas season as a reminder of our need for a Savior. We cannot achieve perfection. A perfect life in how it is centered around our narcissism, perhaps. Our lives may not be like Tiger Woods' at this point, but all of us fall short from time to time. The good news is that because of Jesus, we who anchor ourselves in Him now live as righteous in God's eyes through the perfection of our salvation paid for by Jesus on Calvary. In plainer language, live for Jesus, and in the midst of our striving when we or someone around us falls short in this journey of life, look at Jesus. If you need a role model, imitate Him; and through a relationship with Him, you will get the assistance you need.

Good is Still Predominant in the World
March 5, 2000

This past week has been a gruesome, thought-provoking week in the annals of recent history. On Friday before last, four officers were acquitted in the murder of Amadou Diallo. A six-year-old shot and killed another six-year-old in school. A Pennsylvania man went on a rampage, killing several people and setting his apartment on fire. Events such as these, constantly paraded in local and national news, make many of us afraid to watch television. The human psyche can only take so much bad news.

On one level, society must blame itself for these events. We have created a climate for this type of activity. On another level, we who know Christ should impact the world in such a manner that these occurrences become rare. Unfortunately, in spite of megachurches and multiple ministries, times seem to be getting worse.

There is, however, a better way to view events like the ones of this past week. The Bible, in John 21:25, states, *Jesus did many other things as well. If every one of them were written down, I suppose that even the whole world would not have room for the books that would be written.* The reason we are so shocked and saddened by these events is because of all the good in the world. We take this good for granted, assuming it will always be present. When it is taken away, we react with horror and dismay. Living in the midst of chaos and anarchy isn't normal.

Nevertheless, unfortunate incidents such as these will continue to happen. Jesus reminds us that these are the signs of the last days. They are a present reminder that sin is a reality in the world. Yet, the Bible tells us that *greater is He that is in you than he who is in the world* (1 John 4:4 KJV). The Lord encourages us to do the work of the Church in the world, and while doing so, we are implored to meet needs. We may get discouraged because of the immensity of the challenge; but, in spite of discouragement, we must remember that we already know how the story ends. Jesus wins, and so do we.

What is Your True Name?
May 7, 2010

1 Samuel 25:25a: *My lord, do not take seriously this ill-natured fellow, Nabal; for as his name is, so is he; Nabal is his name, and folly is with him* (NRSV).

One person has the potential to stop a show.

Senator Jim Bunning of Kentucky, in his own brand of wisdom, recently held up a $10 billion bill that would extend unemployment benefits for over a million Americans in this the worst economic climate since the Great Depression. Due to the power of the filibuster, the security of many US citizens was put at risk by a man who opposed one of the few bills in recent memory with true bipartisan support. When asked to reconsider his position, Senator Bunning responded to the person making the request with profanity. This type of behavior isn't new for Senator Bunning, a baseball Hall of Famer, who, in his later years, has become known for his mean demeanor. Time magazine highlighted him as one of the worst senators of 2006.

The Bible tells us of a rich man who was so me-centric that he almost caused his entire household to be murdered due to foolish pride. His name was Nabal, which in Hebrew means "fool," and he lived up to his name. In the story connected to the above text, David and his men protected the servants of Nabal as they took care of their flocks, and asked Nabal for some provisions. Nabal, in turn, insulted them to the point where everyone in the household agreed with David and not Nabal; while David, being insulted, made his way with his soldiers to destroy Nabal's house. Nabal's quick thinking wife saved the household from disaster. Her actions were nearly mirrored by those who implored Senator Bunning to finally back down to avert disaster.

These stories have direct application for us. Have any of us been obstructionists just for the sake of being difficult? Have we stood in the way of a blessing for someone else? Have we taken a stance not because it was right, but because we could? Do we only make decisions based on how they affect us alone? And, when we take our stances, do we ever consult God through God's Word first? Many times what we consider to be a sage and noble position is actually one that a Nabalite would choose.

Our desire should always be to build up and not tear down, to support and not kill. We should want to help others prosper and excel, and seek the best for others and ourselves. The operative word for today is eagle. Soar like an eagle, and avoid being like a crab in a barrel, and I'm certain that God will be pleased. Live in this way, and your true name will be "Christian".

Did You Really Love Me?
July 11, 2010

Today the smoke and heat from the bright fire-cracker display known as, "Where will LeBron James play next season?" is now extinguished. James, an NBA Rookie of the Year out of high school, played the last seven seasons for the Cleveland Cavaliers, which was a bond made stronger by the fact that James is a native of Akron, part of the Cleveland metro area. LeBron has always unabashedly said that his goal was to win championships, and so, in an unprecedented move, he and two other superstars are going to Miami via free agency. For many, this was the most logical choice.

My focus in this space isn't to deal with the pros and cons of James' decision, nor the merits of a special program on ESPN to make the announcement. Rather, there is a teaching moment in the reactions of some Cleveland Cavaliers fans and the team's owner. Moments after James' announcement two interesting things happened. First, several fans decided it was the appropriate time to burn LeBron's Cleveland jersey. Second, the principal owner of the Cavaliers, Dan Gilbert, sent a letter very uncharacteristic of a sports team owner to the local Cleveland newspaper, and said, among other things, "If you thought we were motivated before tonight to bring the hardware to Cleveland, I can tell you that this shameful display of selfishness and betrayal by one of our very own has shifted our 'motivation' to previously unknown and previously never experienced levels. Some people think they should go to heaven but NOT have to die to get there. Sorry, but that's simply not how it works."[xxxvii]

Has anyone ever said they loved you, and then, when you did something they didn't like, turned on you? Have you ever had friends who were in your corner, but who, at the first sign of trouble—or profit for themselves—sold you out? Why is it so easy for us to forget the good things, but develop animosity over the bad things? Most of us who read this will not benefit in any way from LeBron's decision. Basketball, although I'm a great fan, is a sport and recreational entertainment. Yet, sinful nature can show up even here. Think this is overkill? On Palm Sunday, the Jerusalem crowds shouted, "Hosanna!" at the entry of Jesus into town. By that Friday they said, *His blood be on us and on our children* (Matthew 27:25 NRSV). Such is the nature of human beings. Knowing this, we who live transformed lives through Christ should continue to model a different way, a way of grace. This way always leaves room for forgiveness.

Are You in the Lord, or Just in the Church?
August 15, 2010

This past week, a couple, planning to attend church together got into an argument. As a result of their heated words, the husband decided to walk to church. The wife followed him in a car, and ran over him. As of this writing, he is recuperating in the hospital and will be fine. His wife is currently involved in involuntary prison ministry.

Were they arguing about church? About their relationship? About something else? Was this madness inspired by the use of legal or illegal substances? We may never know. This uncommon, uncouth example reminds us of the power of conflict. Unchecked conflict can cause you to do unacceptable things with permanent ramifications. Some conflict also anchors in selfishness; it is one person forcefully imposing their will on another. Although conflict in and of itself isn't bad—it is a transitional state leading to some resolution—it has the potential for causing much grief.

There is another part of the above scenario that is even more troubling than the couple's conflict—they were on their way to church! One could argue that the end result shows that they need church. However, this would be an incomplete view. It is good to be in the Church, but it is better to be in the Lord. This simply means to have a relationship with Jesus Christ. The Church is a vehicle, an organism, to facilitate Christian growth and transformation. What we have done in many churches is introduce fallen humanity to an institution, and then tell them that this is the step necessary to secure salvation. So a person joins a church, sits on a pew, and is the same person ten years from now that they were on that initial day of uniting with that fellowship.

In plain language, the purpose of the Church is to lead and enhance a transformational relationship with Jesus Christ. I dare say that if you join this church for any other reason, you have cheated yourself by merely connecting with an institution and not securing a relationship. If this is you, I hear the question now—"How can this be changed?" The answer is to allow Jesus in your life. Also, attend Bible Study and/or Sunday school so you can grow in your understanding of the Lord. Then, find your place of service in this fellowship, so you can help yourself and others grow in their Christian walk. These actions will transform your life, which is the goal of our relationship with Jesus. Then, you will resist the urge to run over your spouse or your friend on the way to church…

The Celebration of Witnessing
May 29, 2011

Today we observe both Missionary and Senior Citizens Day at First Baptist. We are reminded of the faithful work of missionaries in spreading the good news. Through their perseverance we have a saving knowledge of the Lord. We are blessed, because, as Scripture says, *And these all, having obtained a good report through faith, received not the promise: God having provided some better thing for us, that they without us should not be made perfect.* (Hebrews 11:39-40 KJV).

We also remember the great worth of our elders. The African proverb, "It takes a whole village to raise a child," implies that seniors must be present to provide direction. I fondly remember the influence of my maternal grandmother in reminding me of the past while pushing me toward the future.

Some may ask. "How do missionary activity and the commemoration of senior citizens come together?" During the prime of our seniors' lives, they were not ashamed to tell others about Jesus. It is no accident that in the majority of our churches, seniors make up most of the congregation. Their ability to testify to the goodness of God continues to bear fruit. Our focus in the near future will be on relational evangelism. Many of you are unknowingly practicing this right now; in recent weeks we have had an increase of visitors at our services.

I encourage you to continue to spread the good news of the gospel and this church in the Memphis community.

Remember the words of the Samaritan woman presented to us this past Women's Day, *Come, see a man, which told me all things that ever I did: is not this the Christ?* (John 4:29 KJV) As we view these words, recognize that this woman witnessed to the unconverted. Pray that God will send people who need to know Him in your pathway; you can then lead them to the doors of the church. Continue to let your light shine toward the door of God's lighthouse—the Church.

That Might be Jesus
August 21, 2011

On Monday afternoons I often attended the Baptist Ministers Conference of New York and Vicinity, the largest local conference of Baptist preachers in the country. After the meeting, as we often did, we separated to one of our two gathering places for food and fellowship. I regularly ate with the group at Wilson's restaurant at 158th Street and Amsterdam Avenue. This was a lively corner, in the midst of the 'hood, and the frontage of Wilson's was made up of plate glass windows. The owner of Wilson's made special arrangements on Monday afternoons for the ministers to sit in front of the largest window facing Amsterdam Avenue. From this view we were able to see both the good and bad of New York City.

On one particular Monday, a young man wearing shabby clothes stood in front of our plate glass window. He appeared to be mute, and for a long time he stood before us and stared intensely at our table. After a while, he took out a sketchpad from his knapsack and began to draw. He would sketch a picture of one of us, tap on the window to get our attention, and then hold it up to the window for that person to see. He would then hold out his hand. Of course, none of us commissioned him to create these masterpieces, so we tried to ignore him, and continued to eat. This did not discourage our newfound friend, for he continued to sketch, rap on the window, and hold out his hand.

Finally, one of the older ministers seated at our table spoke. He was a former bodyguard for Malcolm X who had given his life to Christ and was later called to preach. He said to us, "I'm going outside to the brother—that might be Jesus." All of a sudden, forks found a resting place on the plates sitting before them. Glasses were placed on the table. Chairs shifted, bodies moved, doors opened, and the ministers fellowship that moments ago was inside Wilson's was now outside. Minutes later, we returned to our seats with our newly purchased portraits in hand.

Hebrews 13:2: Do not forget to entertain strangers, for by so doing some people have entertained angels without knowing it.

What a Communal Meal could Look Like
September 4, 2011

Luke 14:12-14: *He said also to the one who had invited him, "When you give a luncheon or a dinner, do not invite your friends or your brothers or your relatives or rich neighbors, in case they may invite you in return, and you would be repaid. But when you give a banquet, invite the poor, the crippled, the lame, and the blind. And you will be blessed, because they cannot repay you, for you will be repaid at the resurrection of the righteous* (NRSV).

About three weeks ago, I, along with some of you, attended a unique community meal sponsored by the Lott Carey Baptist Foreign Mission Convention. On the Monday night of the convention, a banquet room in the Cook Convention Center was filled with delegates. Included with that number were over 300 homeless people from all over the city. The theme of the meal was "come as you are," and there was at least one homeless person at each table, so you couldn't identify anyone sitting with you as being homeless or not. I listened to the comments of various people as they left the banquet, and it was clear that they enjoyed everything – the food, the music (by Trio Plus), and the fellowship. The gathering at this banquet is a mirror of heaven, where all get invited. The imagery of the banquet setting described in the Scripture above is, I believe, a reflection of how Jesus wants us to conduct ourselves <u>in the here and now.</u>

Since the Church is an association of people gathered through belief in Jesus Christ, it is always in the mode of receiving more people unto itself. And we who are already here must be in the mode to receive them. If we won't receive Jesus, and therefore can't receive others, we may be on the outside looking in; and an existence without Jesus, whether in this life or the one to come, is a sad existence indeed.

How to Get in Spiritual Shape
December 4, 2011

Watch any television program with commercials and you will probably see at least one ad that deals with the "battle of the bulge." During the next few weeks we will overindulge our eating habits then repent in the New Year by vowing to lose weight by whatever means necessary. This is the rollercoaster that many of us ride during a year.

Getting into shape is not easy. Any healthy means of weight loss will take time, and involve that cuss word known as exercise. But it is necessary. This raises an interesting point for us who know Jesus. The Bible says in 1Timothy 4:8, *For physical training is of some value, but godliness has value for all things, holding promise for both the present life and the life to come.*

During this Christmas season we should seek to get into spiritual shape. As we ponder the Greatest Gift given to us, we should look at our spiritual health. Are we spiritually flabby? Obese? Fit? In order to do this assessment, we must ask a basic question – What is spiritual fitness? One thing that acts as a test for spiritual vitality is something we read every first Sunday before observing the ordinance of the Lord's Supper. I'm referring to the church covenant. When we read it, we see where we should be in our spiritual fitness journey:

- To walk together in Christian love
- To strive for the advancement of this church in knowledge, holiness and comfort

- To promote its prosperity and spirituality
- To contribute regularly and cheerfully to the support of the ministry, the expenses of the church, the relief of the poor and the spread of the gospel throughout all nations
- We also engage to maintain as far as possible family and secret devotion
- To teach our children the Christian truths
- To seek the salvation of our kindred and acquaintances
- To cultivate Christian sympathy in feeling and courtesy in speech
- To be slow to take offense but always ready for reconciliation
- To watch over one another with brotherly love
- To remember each other in prayer
- To aid each other in sickness and distress

It is our responsibility to care for the temple of the body, and to nurture its spirit. One without the other creates imbalance. We must stay committed to the vibrancy of both.

The Problem with Situational Ethics
March 10, 2013

Judges 17:5-6: *Now this man Micah had a shrine, and he made an ephod and some idols and installed one of his sons as his priest. In those days Israel had no king;* ***everyone did as he saw fit.***

The above text comes from the book of Judges, one of the pivotal books of the Old Testament. The context for the passage is given to us in chapter 2, verses 10-12, *After that whole generation had been gathered to their fathers, another generation grew up, who knew neither the Lord nor what he had done for Israel. Then the Israelites did evil in the eyes of the Lord and served the Baals. They forsook the Lord, the God of their fathers, who had brought them out of Egypt. They followed and worshiped various gods of the peoples around them.* This scene reinforces the reality of this book, which goes on to tell us that because of rebellion, God caused them to lose battles they would have normally won. However, because God held true to covenant and relationship with Israel, when they called out for Divine deliverance, God would answer.

Often times when we view Scripture, we sanitize it to glean a general antiseptic truth without accepting the grimy reality that the Bible is often a mirror. It shows us the good, bad and ugly sides of our existence, and causes us to look at ourselves in ways we would rather avoid. So even as we see the behavior of Israel in Judges, we must admit that if we changed the names of the characters, this could be a book written about large segments of the Church in 21st century America. Don't understand? We are guilty of *situational ethics.* In other words, as the text says above, ***everyone did as he saw fit.***

In the text, Micah made up his own religion. Here is a Jew, bound by covenant with God and the law to worship at the Tabernacle, who instead created an idol and *made* one of his sons the priest. Micah's mother, as the Bible tells us in Judges 17:3, gave Micah a portion of some silver that she thought she lost, *but Micah had stolen,* to create the idol that she consecrated to the Lord!

Human limitations cause us to create a religion even within our relationship with Jesus and create idols that loom larger than our relationship with the Lord. We then try to shape the church to fit our concept of our religion, instead of finding out what God would have us to do. In our Christian witness, we have those who speak out against abortion, yet bomb abortion clinics. We also nurture our pet sins, like the case of the man sleeping with his stepmother in 1 Corinthians 5:1-3, but zealously rise against others we don't like. The purpose of Christ's Church is to give us a transformed life through our relationship with Jesus Christ, and we then in turn lead others into the same joyous transformation that we possess. But when we give in to situational ethics, we create our own god while crowding the true God out. The results can be disastrous; Romans 1:28 describes it as God giving us up to a *reprobate mind* (KJV)—that is, God taking Divine hands off of us because that is what we want.

As we walk in this Lenten season, I encourage you to avoid the draw of situational ethics and draw closer to God; and allow Him to pilot your journey, even if it leads to unexpected places.

A Better Use of One's Focus
November 17, 2013

(This piece was also highlighted on *northstarnews.com*)

Romans 14:1-10, 14-15: *Accept him whose faith is weak, without passing judgment on disputable matters. One man's faith allows him to eat everything, but another man, whose faith is weak, eats only vegetables. The man who eats everything must not look down on him who does not, and the man who does not eat everything must not condemn the man who does, for God has accepted him. Who are you to judge someone else's servant? To his own master he stands or falls. And he will stand, for the Lord is able to make him stand. One man considers one day more sacred than another; another man considers every day alike. Each one should be fully convinced in his own mind. He who regards one day as special, does so to the Lord. He who eats meat, eats to the Lord, for he gives thanks to God; and he who abstains, does so to the Lord and gives thanks to God. For none of us lives to himself alone and none of us dies to himself alone. If we live, we live to the Lord; and if we die, we die to the Lord. So, whether we live or die, we belong to the Lord. For this very reason, Christ died and returned to life so that he might be the Lord of both the dead and the living. You, then, why do you judge your brother? Or why do you look down on your brother? For we will all stand before God's judgment seat. Therefore let us stop passing judgment on one another. Instead, make up your mind not to put any stumbling block or obstacle in your brother's way. As one who is in the Lord Jesus, I am fully convinced that no food is unclean in itself. But if anyone regards something as unclean, then for him it is unclean. If your brother is distressed because of what you eat, you are no longer acting in love. Do not by your eating destroy your brother for whom Christ died.*

There exists in the African-American community a push

for a social and religious focus in the political sphere. Simply put, there are those who consider the issues of abortion and same sex marriage to be the pillars of what makes us a nation "formed on Christian principles." Anything or anyone that doesn't meet the Biblical standard, in their opinion, is not only a denial of the faith, but a great disruption to national stability and security. The following words in this space aren't a theological treatise on the validity of a particular stance concerning these two issues. A large portion of the Church today still has little tolerance for abortions or same sex marriage. This even holds true when you consider Christians who are pro choice and who see the public, not religious, use of civil and same sex unions as acceptable. How can this be? Let me show you, as the Bible says, *a more excellent way* (1 Corinthians 12:31 KJV).

The apostle Paul, in both Romans 14:1-15 and 1 Corinthians 8, broaches the subject of eating meat sacrificed to idols. Remember that in the context of much of the ancient world, a stand connected to the back of the pagan temple was the place where many people in cities got their meat. Some converts to the Christian faith couldn't shake the origin of the meat, and became willful vegetarians. Others, who understood that idols had no power, bought the meat and ate it. This created a challenge for those with a more sensitive conscience.

In both Romans and 1 Corinthians, the "enlightened ones" are encouraged to not eat meat in front of those for whom this would be problematic. When you read these texts and attempt to apply them to the issues of abortion and same sex marriage, it appears that the rest of us should change for the sake of those who want a society solely based on Christian principles. One must keep in mind that the primary application of these texts was for Christians in fellowship with each other. They do, however, have some application here; for they recognize the existence of a pluralistic society, and raise the question of how someone should cope in circumstances where people don't share your views. Notice that in our texts the Christians never tried to stop the idol temples from selling meat. Why not? Because their job was to tell the world about Jesus while living their witness.

We cannot legislate people to live as Christians, just as we can't zip off our skin and change ethnicities. We can, however, share and live the gospel, realizing that people have to make the *choice* to follow Jesus for themselves. We must also realize that our witness must become broader than hot button issues that often get raised to take our eyes off of a larger agenda. There are issues in this country that stem from continued racism, poverty, economic disparity, sexism, and food deserts, among others factors. These seemingly get little to no focus from those who emphasize personal piety; but if you read the Word, it gives focus to many of these issues as well.

In the spirit of our text, it is time for the Christian who has concern about these issues to consider these words...*therefore let us stop passing judgment on one another. Instead, make up your mind not to put any stumbling block or obstacle in your brother's way* (Romans 14:13).

CHAPTER EIGHT - STONY THE ROAD WE TROD

Can These Bones Live?
Can Things Change?
Things Slightly Change, While too Much Remains the Same
An Example of Our Rich History
Lift Every Voice and Sing
God Who hast Brought Us thus Far on the Way
Strength in the Present from the Lessons of the Past
A Delayed, Yet Impactful Return
How Cheap is a Black Life These Days?
Blessings from an Improbable Place
Strange Fruit
The Aftermath of an Unjust Outcome
You Are the Man
Do You Think Globally? Do You Have a Diaspora Mindset?
What Is Your Place?

Can These Bones Live?
July 16, 2017

In a world that's fractured and fraying, many look for secure footing. When we take an introspective look into our communities, we see challenges that consistently greet us like a chronic disease. On a personal level, we wrestle with dead ends and disconnects that can't seem to go away. We know that we need healing, but remain in a daze concerning how to get it. Personal and collective healing seems like an impossible task.

In Ezekiel 37, God meets the prophet in a dump full of bones so old that they were bleached, broken, and very dry. God then asks the prophet an interesting question in verse 3, "Can these bones live?" In other words, brother prophet, can the impossible happen? If we're honest, this is how we view some of our personal and collective issues. For us, they are now insurmountable mountains. The issue then becomes how we answer God's question. To say no outright means that the bleached, broken bone yard is acceptable and the status quo is preferable. We can kill and be killed all day long, for example, because it's ok for Black life to be cheap. On the other hand, to say yes causes another question: "Then why haven't you addressed these bones yet?"

In our text, Ezekiel gives the right answer: "O Sovereign Lord, you alone know." That answer released God to make the impossible happen by instructing the prophet on what to say to the bones, and by verse 10 there stood a mighty army created out of the impossible.

There are two simple points we get from our text. First, we must remember and rely on God. If the truth be told, any progress we've made corporately and individually happened due to the providence of God. Seemingly, we've found ways to rely on other means to solve our problems. By the time we realize that these efforts don't work, what we need fixed becomes reduced to bleached, broken bones. It is time to renew and strengthen our connection to the God of our salvation.

Finally, once God instructs us, we must move on those things that heretofore were thought to be impossible. Our mustard seed faith will cause them to move. Then, the words of Ezekiel 37:10 can become a reality:

> *So I prophesied as he commanded me, and breath entered them; they came to life and stood up on their feet—a vast army.*

Can Things Change?
August 24, 1997

There is a saying that "the more things change, the more they stay the same." On July 25th, two white men in Virginia made a decision about the life on an African-American man. One of them said, as stated in the Associated Press, ``We're going to take G.P. out there and put him on that white cross and burn him."[xxxviii] One of them also boasted, ``Have you ever heard of the perfect crime?" Two men, one of them a recent transplant from New York, decided that they would douse Garnett Paul ``G.P." Johnson with fuel, burn him alive, and then behead him with an ax.

Even as we are appalled by this situation, the laws designed to benefit and protect us are not being enforced. For example, Title VI of the Civil Rights Act of 1964 supports nondiscrimination in federally assisted programs. However, we are presently in an era of states' rights, which returns us to a national climate that existed right before the Civil War. In our own state there is renewed controversy over this issue. It appears that African-American communities have been grossly underserved, and the spirit and function of Title VI has been ignored. Movement is underway to file a class action suit through many entities in our community. Our Tennessee Baptist Missionary & Educational Convention has gone on record in support of this legal maneuver.

It is our individual and collective responsibility to address the ills of our society. When we do this, we must remember that the power of God is accessible to assist in this process. It is the power behind the dismantling of Jim Crow and apartheid. It is the force that God gives for the pulling down of strongholds. God has given this power to us so that we will use it. I pray will we use it wisely.

Things Slightly Change, While too Much Remains the Same February 21. 1999

As we continue to walk through Black History Month, we see flashes of the future and the past. In The Bronx, an unarmed African immigrant from the country of Guinea was shot 41 times by four white New York City police officers that were searching for someone else. In Texas, a trial began for the first of three men who tied James Byrd, Jr. to a truck and dragged him nearly three miles until his body was torn to pieces. In an auction house in Los Angeles, the Heisman trophy of O.J. Simpson was sold this week, reminding us of how the mighty can fall.

These incidents are raised in this space not as an irritant, but as a reminder. Every now and then we must rise from the midst of our possessions and realize, as the saying goes, "the more things change, the more they stay the same." Amadou Diallo, the Guinean immigrant, came from a prosperous family. He was buried in Hollande Bouru, a village of 10,000 people founded by his great-grandfather. His father, Saikou Amad Diallo, has set up import-export companies in Liberia, Singapore, Thailand and Togo. Mr. Byrd was a lifelong resident of Jasper, Texas. Mr. Simpson was a sports and cultural icon. Yet these three men, whether by fate or design, found themselves in a situation where their pigment was a liability.

These incidents remind us how we are still perceived by many in society. Diallo was perceived as expendable. On Wednesday, Texas prosecutors in the trial of John William

King,, one of three white men accused of dragging James Byrd, Jr. to his death, said that on that fateful day King did not wear his hatred on his sleeve but wore it all over his body. Prosecutors showed color photographs of dozens of intricate racist, satanic and neo-Nazi tattoos on King's body to the jury. "If you look closely, there's a tree branch and a man hanging from the tree," Rich Ford, a Jasper police detective, testified. "It appears to be a black man hanging from a tree." [xxxix]

However, things have changed. Both The Bronx and Texas incidents have sparked a large outcry from a cross section of society. In addition, several media outlets, especially newspapers, have done in-depth, and in most cases, fair stories on these tragedies. Many people, after seeing the effects of racism, have decided to *beat their swords into plowshares and their spears into pruning hooks* (Isaiah 2:4). Proper resolution of these types of incidents seems much more certain than in times past. The past might have been bleak, and the present at times may be cloudy, but the future is promising because God is yet in control.

We should remember the past so we do not repeat its mistakes. We should walk in the present with our eyes wide open. We then can walk into the future with a God who enables us to do all things. Examples of this are all around us. The positive changes in the African diaspora did not happen by chance; God honored the prayers of those who have gone before, so that they, with us, as Hebrews 11:40 says, *would be made perfect.*

An Example of Our Rich History
February 6, 2000

Today begins the celebration of Black History Month at First Baptist. During this month we will, starting next Sunday, have sermonic emphasis on our history. Many of us will be dressed in African attire. On the third Sunday, our Missionary Society will present a program designed to make our history come alive. History is a great vehicle that helps us to view foundational events. We then are to take the tool of history and navigate into the present. This way we can see how history has shaped our current reality.

The first day of this month is a pivotal date in the life of America. On February 1, 1960, four brave young men, none over twenty, made a history-making decision. On the night before, one of the students sat thinking about discrimination. "Segregation makes me feel that I'm unwanted," Joseph A. McNeil said later in an interview. "I don't want my children exposed to it."[xl] As the *New York Times* later reported, "the 17-year-old student from Wilmington, N. C., said that he approached three of his classmates the next morning and found them enthusiastic over a proposal that they demand service at the lunch counter of a downtown variety store. About 4:45 P.M. they entered the F. W. Woolworth Company store on North Elm Street in the heart of Greensboro. Mr. Joseph said he bought a tube of toothpaste and the others made similar purchases. Then they sat down at the lunch counter. A Negro woman kitchen helper walked up, according to the students, and told them, 'You know you're not supposed to be in here.' She later called them 'ignorant' and a 'disgrace' to their race. The students then asked a white waitress for coffee. 'I'm sorry but we don't serve colored here,' they quoted her. 'I beg your pardon,' said Franklin McCain, 18, of Washington, 'you just served me at a counter two feet away. Why is it that you serve me at one counter and deny me at another. Why not stop serving me at all the counters.' The four students sat, coffee-less, until the store closed at 5:30 P. M.... This began a movement that spread to Virginia, Florida, South Carolina and Tennessee and involved fifteen cities." [xli]

As you moved about this past week, you probably patronized at least one restaurant. You probably gave no thought about your meal or the service. Forty years ago, this was not the case. We have made great strides as a people, but the race is not over. God is calling on us, just as committed Christians heard the call in the past, to be change agents. As we visit our history this month, let us gain strength from the past so we can courageously engage the future.

Lift Every Voice and Sing
February 4, 2001

In the recent past, we heard about a horrible earthquake in India, and an airplane crash in Colorado. These are but two examples of unexpected tragedies that occur all around the globe, every day. We make plans all the time without consideration for the unknown. This is not to say that we should live our lives in fear of tragedy; the Bible tells us that *perfect love casts out fear* (1 John 4:18). It alerts us to the intangible reality of existence.

These occurrences remind us that the rhyme and reason of life is anchored fully in God. As we observe Black History Month, this fact is stamped on our existence as a people in America. If we view the odds, all of the unexpected tragedies of our history should have erased us from the books of time, yet we are still here. We are here because of God. James Weldon Johnson, in the second and third verses of *Lift Every Voice and Sing*, said it best:

Stony the road we trod, bitter the chas'ning rod
Felt in the days when hope unborn had died
Yet with a steady beat, have not our weary feet
Come to the place for which our fathers sighed?
We have come over a way that with tears has been watered
We have come, treading our path through the blood of the slaughtered
Out from the gloomy past, till now we stand at last
Where the white gleam of our bright star is cast.

God of our weary years, God of our silent tears
Thou who has brought us thus far on the way

Thou who hast by Thy might, led us into the light
Keep us forever in the path we pray.
Lest our feet stray from the places, our God, where we met Thee
Lest out hearts, drunk with the wine of the world, we forget Thee
Shadowed beneath Thy hand, may we forever stand
True to our God, true to our native land[xlii]

God Who hast Brought Us thus Far on the Way
February 9, 2003

Black History Month began as Negro History Week when it was founded by Carter G. Woodson in 1926. It was initially created enhance the knowledge of Black History, and placed during February in honor of the birthdays of Frederick Douglas and Abraham Lincoln. As we begin our formal observance of this month at First Baptist, this past week shows us that our history is not stationary but ever changing and evolving. This past Wednesday at the United Nations headquarters in New York, Secretary of State Colin Powell, the son of Jamaican immigrants, born a few miles from the UN headquarters, presented the United States' case against Iraq. Kofi Annan, a native son of Ghana, heard Powell's information in his role as the Secretary-General of the United Nations. Heavily weighing in on the Bush administration's policies was the National Security Advisor, Dr. Condoleezza Rice, a daughter of the South.

Regardless of how we may feel about the President's policies and the specter of war, people of African descent are engaged in the process involving our world's future. Just a few years ago this would be unthinkable. In light of this, it is time for us to realize two things. First, we are a people whose travels; since the time of the Phoenicians, the Olmecs of Mexico, and the Moors, have created a diaspora of people around the globe. We must acknowledge and begin to operate in this worldwide connectedness. Second, the nation and the world are now multicultural, and we must begin to use the gains of civil rights to create economic power for our people.

All of this must be undergirded with the "faith of our fathers" so these realities will work our best interest. Collectively, whether through lewd lifestyles or consumerism, whether sanctimonious or secular, we have left God out of our proceedings as a people since the time of King; and we presently reap the aftermath of the whirlwind. As we commemorate this Black History Month, let's remember the role of God in our history. The same God that walked with us out of slavery, Jim Crow, and Civil Rights, now walks with us in the present. If we remember God, God's presence will go with us into our future.

Strength in the Present from the Lessons of the Past
April 4, 2004

Soon I will be done with the troubles of this world, troubles of this world, troubles of this world. Soon I will be done with the troubles of this world; I'm going home to live with God.

The previous words are part of a Negro spiritual. They echo the sentiments of a people constantly living under the firm heel of slavery. Living in a situation that appeared to be hopeless, they anchored their sights to the hereafter, the eternal. They realized that the "troubles of this world" were temporary, and eternity would be timeless continuity.

In our day we often move to dismiss the past. It is true that we should not lift up the past merely because it exists, but it does have lessons for us. As we look at these words from the past we must ask the question, "How should we deal with trouble?" First, we must recognize that trouble don't last always. This is what enabled a people in chains to realize that their situation would change. They looked forward and saw the completion of that change in their descendants—us. David said it best when, after his punishment from God due to his disobedience, he said, *weeping may endure for a night, but joy cometh in the morning* (Psalm 30:5 KJV).

Second, we must turn our troubles over to God. One of the reasons for our spiritual strength was a conversation with Jesus. We are encouraged in various portions of

Scripture to give our problems to God. In the final analysis, God can handle them better that we can.

Finally, we must ask God for direction when presented with trouble. As we view the words of this Negro spiritual, a plea for direction is not obvious but implied. When viewing the Black church in relation to slavery, many people feel that it only points to eternity without addressing the present, thus it's of "no earthly good." These words also point to a practical, tangible reality that became obvious with succeeding generations. The Underground Railroad and the Civil Rights Movement, among other examples, show us that faith without works is dead. We have trouble all around us. Perhaps God sometimes allows us to be in the midst of trouble because at some point, God wants us to be a part of the solution, not the problem. And maybe in the middle of our personal problems God wants the world to see how a Christian continues to trust Him, therefore seeing a living example of a Christian walk.

Today we enter the most solemn period on the Christian calendar. It is generally known as Holy Week. On this day Jesus enters triumphantly into a rejoicing Jerusalem. By Thursday, He observes the Passover with His disciples, partially in preparation for the cross. During that night Jesus is taken into custody, abused, humiliated and sentenced to death. By 12 noon on Friday, He hangs on a cross between two heinous and convicted criminals. Sometime after 3 pm on Friday Jesus' remains are placed in a borrowed tomb. Then Sunday arrives, with the borrowed tomb bereft of its occupant. He is risen! Because of this, trouble for the Christian is like the bodily dirt of the day;

due to the cleansing blood of Jesus it is eventually washed away.

A Delayed, Yet Impactful Return
July 19, 2009

Hebrews 11:39-40: *Yet all these, though they were commended for their faith, did not receive what was promised, since God had provided something better so that they would not, apart from us, be made perfect* (NRSV).

I got shoes, you got shoes
All of God's chillum got shoes
When I get to heaven I'm gonna put on my shoes
I'm gonna walk all ovah God's heaven
—Negro spiritual

Lost in the continuous nosiness that passes for news these days is an event that many thought they would never live to see. The first American President of African descent, accompanied by his wife, the great-granddaughter of slaves, and their children, walked a few days ago into Cape Coast, a Dutch slave fort on the coast of Ghana, West Africa. This part of the African continent is the ancestral home of many people of African descent in the Western Hemisphere. It undoubtedly was a moving experience for many, including me, as we watched our First Family visit this place of so much pain.

It is not accidental that the descendants of slaves were able to return to the last piece of African soil that perhaps their ancestors once occupied. God answers all prayers, but as the above text suggests, some requests receive the stamp, "Wait." This, many times, is unacceptable to the modern, hurried mind, used to getting things with minimal delay or fuss. Everything, from some of our theology to some of our conversations, kicks against anything that hints at delayed gratification. Yet, that is where God sometimes places us.

People of African descent across the diaspora have raged and rebelled against the trans-Atlantic slave trade from its beginning, even during the rides on the slave ships. We've survived Jim Crow, Mau Mau, apartheid, and various other indignities. Yet, God saw fit for us to view the day when someone from our background—the First Family—the most powerful political representatives of the most powerful country on Earth, could remind us just how far the Lord has brought us. This is the fulfillment of the slave, who, barefoot, longed for the day of freedom through the symbolism of shoes. It is what Dr. Martin Luther King, Jr. talked about when he said, "I may not get there with you, but we as a people will get to the Promised Land."

The skeptic questions why God would have us wait for what should be ours, and suffer through what shouldn't be our lot in life. An answer to this is found in the natural proclivity of humans to veer from the good and embrace the bad. In the midst of this dance between good and evil, God sometimes allows time to play a part in ultimate redemption. This is what allows sinners to become saints saved by grace. Because of this, a few days ago, Barack, Michelle, Malia, and Sasha Obama walked through the "door of no return" in Cape Coast, Ghana; and were able to come *back* through that very same door.

How Cheap is a Black Life These Days?
October 4, 2009

How cheap is a Black life these days? Don't understand what I mean? During the Middle Passage, black "cargo" was unceremoniously dumped into the Atlantic for various reasons. Later, untrained slaves would be killed if they ran away or were insubordinate. Today, if a Black person is killed unjustly by law enforcement, the lost life, unless famous, makes no difference to anyone except the victim's family. Across America, thousands of Black people die because of senseless violence. How many lives no longer exist due to "reckless eyeballing," or being in the wrong place at the wrong time? Outside of the sensationalism on the local evening news, using the fodder of Black lives they really don't care about to boost ratings, life rolls on.

Last week we were again confronted with the true value of a Black life. A God loving, church going 16-year-old honor student was beaten by several youths and left for dead by his perpetrators. The attack occurred when the victim, Derrion Albert, was on his way home from school. He was doing no wrong; he wasn't fighting nor involved in any negative activity, but a young man with a long 2 by 4 board hit him in the back of the head. This started the process that cost young Derrion his life. For the majority of this society, his death gave his life value only because someone videotaped his beating and the video made its way to a local television station. Additional value was added because Derrion was a good student and a model citizen.

So, if it doesn't make television, it isn't happening—that's how many people think. Actually, scenes like the one involving Derrion happen every day all over America, but because Black life is cheap, we are not moved to action. It is time to address what is happening in many of our communities, and leave the "us vs. them" mentality behind. It indeed is the best of times and the worst of times for Black people.

Let me offer a few suggestions on how to counteract the low value that is placed on Black lives. Start with young people. Help the youth in your family, nuclear and extended, to know and understand their worth and encourage them to reach their full potential. Charity ought to begin at home, and then spread abroad. Then look at the youth in your neighborhood, community, and churches, and lend a helping hand. We can talk about our youth all we want: calling them savage and lost, getting tired of asking them to pull up their pants, and blaming them every chance we get, but the facts are that they developed their debauchery, real or perceived, from us. A sapling grows into a straight or crooked tree because of its nurturance; if it is crooked, you can't blame it, for its job is merely to grow.

I applaud all the churches, including ours, that attempt every week to do something to address the value of our lives in the neighborhoods around them. It is also true that we must address the value of our collective lives as Black people, because no one else but us can determine its worth.

Blessings from an Improbable Place
March 28, 2010

Judges 7:7, 12: *Then the LORD said to Gideon, "With the three hundred that lapped I will deliver you, and give the Midianites into your hand. Let all the others go to their homes." The Midianites and the Amalekites and all the people of the east lay along the valley as thick as locusts; and their camels were without number, countless as the sand on the seashore* (NRSV).

We sit about a week removed from the showdown, delivering to America something that took almost 100 years to bring to life. The first plans for universal health care began with President Theodore Roosevelt, a Republican. Several presidents, including Franklin Delano Roosevelt, Harry Truman, Richard Nixon and William Jefferson Clinton, were unable to move this concept forward, although Lyndon Johnson was able to add Medicaid to the nation's healthcare bouquet. But, here we are today, with a Black President and a healthcare bill that seemed improbable just a few weeks ago

We also see violence and threats toward elected officials at an unacceptable and all time high. The term 'Tea Party," once associated with an emancipatory movement that helped to birth our country, is now used by those who could be seen by some as extremists, and seen by others as the newest incarnation of hoods and white sheets. To say that these threats are wrong, regardless of political persuasion is obvious. They merely remind us that the sinfulness of racism, though cloaked under the veneer of a bill, is very vibrant and present.

Our text reminds us that when Israel needed help in a period bereft of leadership, they cried out and God heard them. However, God answered in an unusual way. God told Gideon to fight the Midianites. Then, after Gideon assembled a fighting force of 32,000 men against an army who gathered in the valley "as thick as locusts," God whittled the number down to 300! Through the power of God, this small army was able to vanquish a much larger one. Taking this analogy to the present day, which of the following two concepts, in recent memory was more implausible—an African- American president, or a healthcare bill? Because of a God that can accomplish the impossible, we have a healthcare bill, which several previous presidents could not bring to life, through an African-American one whom a short time ago many of us thought we would never have. The point is that God majors in the impossible all the time.

As we view the events of last week, remember that God made it possible, and God's miracles aren't confined only to this issue. God has miracles for our lives and our community's struggles that connect with His ultimate plan. It is our task to seek what God would have us do, and then walk in it. The journey may be hard, but the rewards are great.

Oh...and regarding our president...the best is yet to come.

Strange Fruit
September 25, 2011

Strange fruit. You can't eat it. You can't use it. So why do you need it? It's necessary because it sends a message. This fruit once walked the earth like you and I, but it became strange because in the end it hung from a tree that was not its natural home.

We live during a time when the information highway moves at the speed of light, yet our ability to trust and access the truth is seemingly worse. Currently, many of the people who look like us provide fodder for the Prison Industrial Complex, and when it becomes expedient, one of us is singled out to become strange fruit. This was the lot of Troy Davis, who, although he committed criminal acts, has not been proven to be a murderer. But, when you need a message to be sent, that doesn't matter.

2011 is an interesting year concerning legal rulings in the court of public opinion. We saw a woman who was probably guilty of killing her child, but, due to technicalities in the legal system, is currently free and lives among us. Conversely, the same legal system legally murdered a man in a case where the witnesses recanted their statements, and there was no DNA or other physical evidence linking him to the crime.

In doing a cursory look at the miracles of Jesus, an important trend becomes clear. To the paralytic on his bed of affliction—rise up and walk; to the man with the withered hand—stretch out your hand; at the feeding of the 5,000—bring the food to me, and after my prayer, pass it out.

When we move into the book of Acts, Peter says to a man born without the ability to walk, 'Silver and gold aren't mine right now, but what I have I freely give, and in Jesus' name its yours—get up and start walking.' Notice anything?

Strange fruit is making a comeback, because some who have never given up their liking for it are promoting its taste. We live on the benefits of the Civil Rights Movement, yet much of our conversation sounds like pre-1955.

We complain, and then wait on God. However, very plainly, in the examples cited above, God moves when we move in faith. Maybe it's time to pray and act. The direction is obvious. God is on our side, and the tools are in our hands. We can either shape the collective palate of our society to eat apples, grapes, pears, oranges, and the like; or prepare to eventually be a part of the strange fruit menu.

The Aftermath of an Unjust Outcome
July 21, 2013

(This piece was also highlighted on *northstarnews.com*)

Saturday night. July 13, 2013. Not guilty. A young man, an African-American 17 year old young man, was walking home from the store, during a time when people walked their dogs and did their evening jog. He was shot by a man who, when he called the police dispatcher, was told to stay in his car. This made sense because he was a part of neighborhood watch, not security or law enforcement.

When I heard the verdict, I was angry, disillusioned, disgusted, but not surprised. The Scottsboro Boys, Emmitt Till, and personal incidents of racial indignities flashed in my mind. A segment of this country still doesn't believe, even after decades of empirical evidence, that these incidents continue to happen. In listening to the national interview of juror B37, for example, we see that the victim is often viewed with a level of blame equal to or greater than the perpetrator's. This points to the composition of the jury, which in my mind put victory in the hands of the defense before the trial began.

The post-racial society that the media convinces us is real is but a rigged shell game. The truth is, as of this writing, there exists several cases that but for some additional publicity, would trouble our national consciousness as much as the death of Trayvon Martin has done. And this particular case needed a national public outcry in order for George Zimmerman to even be arrested for murder on

April 11th, *two months* after the incident happened on February 26th.

The reality is that racial profiling exists. National, state and local studies over the last ten years prove that judgment based on the color of one's skin is alive and well. In West Virginia, Illinois, and New York City, African-Americans find themselves subjected to more stops and searches than whites. On the other side of this same coin, due to societal realities and our own devalued sense of ourselves, several of our communities have become killing fields, with many of us being held hostage.

Perhaps the greatest tragedy out of this verdict is the harsh reminder that since 1955, employees have had raises and cost of living increases, and the minimum wage has gone up several times, but the societal value of a Black man's life remains the same. Let dogfights happen in a home you own? Go to jail. But get caught "breathing while black" in the wrong place? We will be talking about you in the past tense. Meanwhile, the perpetrator receives a "get out of jail free" card; and his gun, the murder weapon, is returned to him.

In viewing this landscape, I'm reminded of King Jehoshaphat in 2 Chronicles 20. He and the kingdom of Judah found themselves in a potential war against superior forces. What did they do? By verse 4 they gathered from across Judah while fasting and paused to hear from God.

What?!!!!!

Think about how far we've come, and think about Who brought us this far. In recent years, with increased freedoms, we have tended to forget about the One who made our victories possible. Even in the aftermath of this tragedy, the vast infrastructure in African-American life remains anchored in the church. The Church encourages us, molds us, and sometimes disappoints us, but it is God's vehicle for connection, empowerment, and transformation.

A key observation comes in the following passage from 2 Chronicles 20, found in verses 15-17: *He said: "Listen, King Jehoshaphat and all who live in Judah and Jerusalem! This is what the Lord says to you: 'Do not be afraid or discouraged because of this vast army. For the battle is not yours, but God's. Tomorrow march down against them. They will be climbing up by the Pass of Ziz, and you will find them at the end of the gorge in the Desert of Jeruel. You will not have to fight this battle. Take up your positions; stand firm and see the deliverance the Lord will give you, O Judah and Jerusalem. Do not be afraid; do not be discouraged. Go out to face them tomorrow, and the Lord will be with you.'"*

We can get two things from this text. The first is that God will fight your battles. Even in this dark hour, God hasn't left us. The second is less obvious, but very present. Notice the word the people receive from the Lord. Although the battle belongs to God, and they won't have to fight, they must still show up! They are to dress, position themselves, and be ready.

We have "stand your ground" laws in 22 states, including Tennessee. We must dress, position ourselves against these laws, and be ready. The 16th largest economy, by spending, exists in Black America. Why can't we harness our consumerism into an economic powerhouse? The killing fields in our communities will change because of our efforts. We must dress, position ourselves and be ready. The systemic poisons designed to kill us must be quarantined. We must dress, position ourselves and be ready: and when we trust and allow God to then do what we can't, we will see the conceptual valuation of a Black life become much more precious and respected.

You Are the Man
July 28, 2013

(This piece was also highlighted on *northstarnews.com*)

Samuel 12:1-7a: *The Lord sent Nathan to David. When he came to him, he said, "There were two men in a certain town, one rich and the other poor. The rich man had a very large number of sheep and cattle, 3 but the poor man had nothing except one little ewe lamb he had bought. He raised it, and it grew up with him and his children. It shared his food, drank from his cup and even slept in his arms. It was like a daughter to him. "Now a traveler came to the rich man, but the rich man refrained from taking one of his own sheep or cattle to prepare a meal for the traveler who had come to him. Instead, he took the ewe lamb that belonged to the poor man and prepared it for the one who had come to him."David burned with anger against the man and said to Nathan, "As surely as the Lord lives, the man who did this deserves to die! He must pay for that lamb four times over, because he did such a thing and had no pity." Then Nathan said to David, "You are the man!...*

On July 19th, President Barack Obama shared with the nation a historical speech focused around the death of Trayvon Martin and the aftermath of the George Zimmerman verdict. There has been a range of responses to what was said, but many were positive. What was most important, in my opinion, was the focus of what was said. It gave the perspective of a people long dismissed in a good portion of the public's discourse, and in its presentation caused the nation to look in a collective mirror. This is a view that it often resists.

Listening to the President caused me to reflect on a biblical incident of needed conversation and confrontation found in 2 Samuel 12:1-7. Here we find the prophet Nathan sent by God to tell the most powerful man in Israel an important message. David needed to know that he had shed innocent blood in order to indulge in illicit pleasures. How do you tell a king who can have you killed that he is wrong? You tell a story that resonates with human decency and fairness. And on that fate-filled Friday, the nation's first African-American President told a portion of his story. You may argue that the President's position is functionally and logistically exclusive from that of a prophet. Yet, the unexpected first African-American President gave a commentary about an unexpected tragedy in which he has some personal experience.

In the above text, Nathan, the prophet, finds that the best way to challenge the one who's wrong is to tell a story in which a poor family has a small, young lamb that, instead of being raised for dinner, became a prized pet. The rich man in this story overlooks his vast resources, and takes this personal possession from the poor family. This is the story shared with King David who, because of his background and innate sense of right versus wrong, immediately became upset and wanted a harsh sentence placed on this insensitive rich man.

We don't always want to see what's wrong with us. We especially don't want to see it when it comes from a source that we should, but don't, respect. Yet, in the biblical story and in the comments by the President, we hear from someone who has the mandate through his position to "'say a word." The Lord sent Nathan, and the people sent

President Obama. The message from both is the same – you are the man. America, in many ways, through only recognizing 3/5 of a person; through lynchings, Jim Crow, unjust drug laws and sentencing, and racial profiling; through Emmett Till, Oscar Grant III, Willie Turks, James Byrd, Yusef Hawkins and Amadou Diallo – you are the man. You couldn't hear it when countless others told you, when empirical evidence told you, but now you might hear the message for the first time.

America, now that you know that you are the man, what are you going to do about it? The key is in your response, and it seems that your response remains stuck in the land of "I'll do what I want because I can." The poor man who owned the ewe lamb was not considered, and his plight didn't count. Yet God sent the prophet for the purposes of self-awareness and repentance.

The Bible, in the beginning of Romans 8:28, tells us that *all things work together for good, to them that love God* (KJV). Maybe if we truly love God, we will use this unfortunate death and prophetical confrontation from an unlikely source to repent and start the process of right-living. True healing requires it, and those who share the plight of the poor man in our text cannot merely be content with being quiet, but must persevere with a purpose.

It's a Great Thing to Finally Wake Up
July 17, 2016

Over the course of time, injustices enacted because of the hue of a person's complexion became unbearable. Time after time, in hamlets all over our country, "Aunt Hagar's children" died at the hands of those who pledged to protect and serve. The perpetrators of these crimes either had their cases dismissed, or were acquitted after a sham of a trial.

One day, the people kissed by the sun had enough, and began protesting for their rights. Those who benefited most from inequity took issue with the protestors, and became nervous at this new position of assertiveness they wielded. Some clergy suggested long seasons of prayer, so that God would move the pendulum without this type of human intervention. Some, who were Black themselves, thought that there could be gradual accommodation allowing things to change over time. Collegial clergy fell out with each other over what took place, some feeling that the blocking of a bridge was an irresponsible use of time and should never happen. Others took issue with the young people leading the marches, saying they could use their time better than to rabble rouse.

If you assumed that what you've read so far was an apt description of the responses from last Sunday's blockage of I-40 by up to 4,000 protesters spawned by the Black Lives Matter Movement, you would be *very* wrong. The first two paragraphs apply to the Civil Rights Movement of the 1950's and '60's, and the bridge was the Edmund Pettis in Selma, Alabama, where at least two members of our congregation marched on what we now know as Bloody Sunday. Because of this civil disobedience, we now have the Voting Rights Act. And now history presents us with a chance to complete tasks left unfinished from 50 years ago.

We are now seeing a watershed moment in our city and country. Memphis, especially, has been groggier than Rip Van Winkle in not addressing some critical needs of its majority population. What you see now is the result that comes from pent up frustration denied for so long.

The days ahead will be interesting. Understand that there will be fits and starts, and we are in the middle of seeing sausage being made – never a pretty process. But, just as we had the bridge blocked, we also saw the interim Police Director lock arms in solidarity with the protestors. Gangs that normally fought each other walked together, as one of their own gave positive instructions. The driver of a tractor-trailer that was blocked by the march allowed protesters to get on top of the truck. And the next day, those protestors got Mayor Jim Strickland to do what several persons were unable to do – meet with them, albeit publicly, instead of sending a minion.

Oh, and at the end of a march made up of 4000 "salt of the earth" people – most of them kissed by the sun – nobody got hurt. In the midst of all of this, I believe, God has a plan; and what better place to have real change than Memphis.

Do You Think Globally?
Do You Have a Diaspora Mindset?
October 1, 2017

Recently, in viewing current events, it's become obvious once again that there is an increased need for global knowledge and perspective. Hurricanes Harvey, Irma and Maria exposed many of us to lands we've never heard of: Barbuda, St. Maarten, and Tortola, among others. This reinforced itself during forecasts for these storms, for most of them emphasized where places in the U.S.A. would be impacted, but gave scant mention to other places directly in the path of these storms.

I may be more sensitive to it than many because I'm the child of immigrants. Many people know I was born and raised in The Bronx, but when they find out that my parents were Jamaican, some ask, "What was it like growing up in Jamaica?" That's when I hear the sound effect of a scratched vinyl record in my head. With some of them, I've then shared that I was born and raised in The Bronx, and they ask the same question again! Once, I responded to the question by asking the native Memphian, "What was it like growing up in Chicago?" They then—slowly—got my point.

Our president's initial indifference toward Puerto Rico, and which continues toward the U.S. Virgin Islands, is reinforced due to many not realizing that these places are commonwealths of the U.S.A., hence a part of our country. This plays itself out in deadly ways. Congress, unlike its swift action in helping Houston and Florida, hasn't, as of this writing, acted in voting to provide assistance for

Puerto Rico and the U.S. Virgin Islands. Celebrities and relatives of those affected have been the major contributors spearheading relief efforts. And the 45th president this past week concentrated on the physicality of the NFL, and the need for players who protest in the spirit of Colin Kaepernick to be fired. Puerto Rico was an afterthought until the groundswell prompted him to move toward action.

Why do I mention these things? Not having a global perception can cost us. Being concerned only for oneself can be deadly. What happened in Houston and what's developing in Puerto Rico are actually man made calamities begun through natural disasters. Unchecked development in Houston that didn't consider natural drainage gave water nowhere to go, and economic issues that preceded the storm in Puerto Rico—created in part by indifference—now has an entire island without electricity. These factors shaped the crisis we now see.

Perception causes us to ask crazy questions, and the inability to listen causes us to stay stuck in erroneous assumptions. We then stand in danger of doing two of the things God hates from Proverbs 6:19—spreading a false witness and pouring out lies, and stirring up dissension among brothers. It's time to see ourselves as a diaspora, with family spread over North, Central and South America; from the Caribbean to Africa and throughout the world. That is the legacy that's been dealt, and we will prosper through learning about and listening to each other.

What Is Your Place?
March 8, 2015

Scandal is a popular TV show described as a political drama loosely based on Judy Smith, a former White House press aide and current CEO of a Washington D.C. crisis management firm. The lead actress, Kerry Washington, plays Olivia Pope, whose background mirrors that of Judy Smith to a large degree. *Scandal* is the brainchild of Shonda Rhimes, writer and executive producer of the "Thank God It's Thursday" television juggernaut which includes the shows *Grey's Anatomy* and *How to Get Away with Murder.* Watching *Scandal* is a rollercoaster ride, along with being many a person's guilty pleasure. But the episode this past week shifted the dynamic, bringing the entertainment value of a TV show much closer to the realities of its huge Black global fan base.

"The Lawn Chair" is an episode based to a large degree on recent events. A young man is gunned down by a police officer and left lying in the street. His father, from the midst of a gathering crowd, moves to his unattended son and fires a licensed shotgun in the air. He refuses to move until justice takes place for his son. By this time the main character, Olivia Pope, who is also Black, intervenes enough to prevent the father from being shot. Her language to the commanding officer is interesting, as she points out all the cameras and cell phones recording the event live. Later information reveals that the police had received word that a Black male had just stolen a cell phone from a nearby business. The son, walking home, had a brand new cell phone in his hand. He was shot because he allegedly pulled a knife and lunged at the officer.

Subsequent videotape showed the young man reaching in his pocket, but it purposely only told part of the story. As the episode unfolded, it was revealed that he was clearly framed with a knife after his death. In this episode, echoes of the Mike Brown, Eric Garner, and Trayvon Martin incidents present themselves, replaying them for many who watched with tears and angst.

This episode masterfully dealt with two sides of the issue of police brutality—from the side of government and law enforcement, with its wrinkles, good and bad. It showed a President wanting to but not addressing this shooting that took place blocks from the White House, due to political expediency. It also gave a glimpse into the mindset of a rogue police officer, and other aspects of police work—especially one view of crowd control. We also saw in this episode the side of the victim. After setting the context and background, this side is what I wish to discuss.

I saw three aspects, perspectives, or players—use whichever term you feel fits best—in this episode on the side of the victim; the "Black" side. First, there was the victim and his family, represented by the father. Many of our people find themselves at one time or another in this place. Next, there was the activist. He stirred up the crowd, while also having the ability to talk to the family. Finally, there was the well-connected go-between, represented by Olivia Pope, who can navigate all worlds; eventually helping to bring about a satisfactory conclusion.

While watching this episode, some may think that this is merely genius in scriptwriting, but the truth is that much of what we enjoy as Black people in this land is the result of a comprehensive effort made up of protest, political leverage, lawsuits and legislation. This episode, however, shows us a present-day solution while revisiting, in its own way, the past. The main takeaway is that everyone involved in this scenario *has a role.* The success at the end of the episode happened because the persons in each aspect, or role, worked together while *remaining in their role.* What does that mean? The father maintained his posture in wanting justice, but yielded when necessary to the other two players so they could play their parts in bringing it to pass. The activist at first didn't appreciate the go-between, but then understood that he and the go-between were on the same team but had different *roles.* The go-between learned that at certain points she had to fall back and be a part of the overall movement, even with her formidable connections. Because each of them played their role, justice took place.

In real life and in real time, many of us forget this rule. No one signs up to be the victim or the victim's family; this comes through circumstance. We become attracted to the limelight surrounding the activist, while forgetting to serve. And if we are blessed to have connections and influence that can help the greater good, we refuse to use them, or squander the opportunity by getting trinkets with temporary shelf life for ourselves. Then, after the smoke from the present problem clears, we wonder why things haven't shifted much, if at all. I submit that this happens because we forget that we all have a place. Some of us are foot soldiers, some can strategize. Others can speak truth to power, educating the masses. We all have a place, yet we often look in envy at the gifts of others. We build personal brands from the misfortune and misery of our people, but wonder why things don't change. Why wonder? As we get involved in our church and our community, through prayer and activity, I'm convinced that each of us will find our place.

Knowing your place, and realizing that we all have a place, will release us from the spinning wheels of the last few years. The Bible says it best in 1 Corinthians 12:24-26:

> *But God has combined the members of the body… so that there should be no division in the body, but that its parts should have equal concern for each other. If one part suffers, every part suffers with it; if one part is honored, every part rejoices with it* (NIV).

We all play a part in our deliverance. What is your place?

CHAPTER NINE - WHY GOD? WHAT IS THE ANSWER?

Where is God?
The Need for God in Trying Times
Watch the Pendulum and Trust God
A View on Suffering
Where to Put Burdens in the Midst of Confusion
Watchfulness in Uncertain Times
An Example of the Power of God
A Bad Number
Hang in There — God is With You
The Ruler of Oceans, Stars and Sky

Where is God?
March 12, 2017

Where is God? If we're honest, there have been times when we've asked this question. The escalating murder rate in our city, along with other senseless incidents, causes many of us to cry out to God. Yet, things seem to get worse. The same could be said for incidents in our personal lives, where we cry out to God with seemingly no response.

Where is God? On vacation? Nonexistent?

We don't make our doubts public, but our private thought life, if we're not careful, will allow our unanswered doubts to make us hollow practitioners of something we don't really believe. Instead of a Christian, we would then be a church member without faith or a relationship with God. To be clear—having doubts on occasion is healthy and happens to all of us. How we wrestle and resolve doubt is the issue.

Where is God?

To answer the question, we must acknowledge something in how humans were and are shaped in interaction with God and the world. Out of all of God's creation, we have the ability to chart our own course and manipulate that which God placed in the world. No other species has the ability to alter the earth's landscape like we do. In addition to this, God gave us one other unique trait that even the angels don't have. God created free will for us as a part of the world's undergirding fabric. In other words, all of us have the freedom to do right or wrong. The issues we see and the challenges we face most times don't begin with God, but start with choices made by us or someone else. The subsequent check then comes due, and it doesn't care who pays it. Adam and Eve, and Cain and Abel happened due to choice, not God.

Where is God?

God walks with us through the pain. Note the scenario with Shadrach, Meschach, and Abednego. The fire they met was made seven times hotter—so hot that the people who threw them into it died. Yet God didn't take them *out* of the fire, God met them *in* the fire, and kept the effects *of* the fire away from them—no smell of smoke, no burning, no death. What is the takeaway? God often walks with us *in* situations while *removing* the sting *of* situations. In spite of tough circumstances, we persevere because God is with us.

Finally, God feels the pain of our situations. God understands temptation, and God understands hurt. Jesus understood the pain of seeming separation on the cross from His Father, and understands how we feel. These verses of Scripture put it best:

> *Therefore, since we have a great high priest who has gone through the heavens, Jesus the Son of God, let us hold firmly to the faith we profess. For we do not have a high priest who is unable to sympathize with our weaknesses, but we have one who has been tempted in every way, just as we are—yet was without sin* (Hebrews 4:15-16).

Where is God? God is where you are. Now that you know, will you choose to trust God?

The Need for God in Trying Times
August 11, 1996

We currently sit in a period of time which is pregnant with peril. Within a month, we have seen the tragedies of TWA flight 800, which was destined for Paris, and the bombing of Centennial Olympic Park in Atlanta during the Olympic games. In both cases, innocent people perished, family units were broken, and lives were irreparably damaged and will never be the same. When we add these events to the rash of church burnings in our part of the country, as well as the increase of crime in our city, a dismal portrait of the future emerges in the minds of many.

People often blame God for these heinous acts. They reason that if God doesn't totally eradicate them, at least God can, in some way, be more selective in who survives them, and who dies. However, we must assign blame where it belongs. God, from the time of Adam and Eve, has given humans free choice. We have, for the most part, abused it. Global warming, erratic weather caused by pollution, high crime, murder, racism, sexism, and any other "ism" you choose, are not God's fault. This blame must sit squarely on our collective shoulders. Free will, used for self-aggrandizement as a result of low self-esteem, caused our two recent bombings.

In this critique of humankind, the Church is most crucial. God, working through the Church, uses it as a hospital for the broken, flawed and frail. It is a vehicle of healing for all. Through the Church, the message of Christ is transmitted to the world. Because of this, we must share the healing and hope that we have received in the church with the rest of humanity. Instead of being influenced by the world, our mission is to lead the world to knowledge of and reconciliation with God. This is what makes evangelism so important in the life of the Church.

In the 14th chapter of Exodus, the Israelites found themselves in a critical situation. They had just left slavery in Egypt, and now they found themselves with the Red Sea in front of them, hills to the left and right, and the Egyptian army closing in to their rear. They cried out to Moses in their distress, and he reassured them. Yet, even Moses had his doubts. In verses 15 and 16, God tells Moses, *Wherefore criest thou unto me? speak unto the children of Israel, that they go forward: But lift thou up thy rod, and stretch out thine hand over the sea, and divide it: and the children of Israel shall go on dry [ground] through the midst of the sea* (KJV).

These words from God are instructional for us. Many times we may see external realities and become discouraged. Remember, however, that God has given us gifts and opportunities with which we can claim the future. This will happen as we follow God's lead. Our future as Christians is always bright, because we always have God. Since we have God, we can change the world around us for good, if we trust Him; and I believe that God wants to change the world partially through this trust. I am reminded of these words coined by Dr. Gary V. Simpson, "Prayer changes me–a changed me changes things."

Watch the Pendulum and Trust God
July 5, 1998

Many items have highlighted the news over the past few weeks. The Monica Lewinsky saga, fueled by the media and our "need to know", just won't die. International diplomacy, and the lack thereof, is being pursued by several nations, including ours. Domestic issues that emphasize the continued reality of racism abound.

In our study of the book, *The Celebration of Discipline*, we are told in the chapter on meditation that we should meditate on current events. A major part of this involves viewing the world with "a Bible in one hand and the newspaper in the other."[xliii] From time to time this is exactly what we attempt to do in this space. In the spirit of this focus, read an excerpt from the following bill, presented recently to Congress:

> **March 4, 1998: This Act may be cited as the "Anti-Discrimination in College Admissions Act of 1998".** ***No institution of higher education that participates in any program authorized under the Higher Education Act of 1965 shall, in connection with admission to such institution, discriminate against, or grant preferential treatment to, any person or group based in whole or in part on the race, sex, color, ethnicity, or national origin of such person or group.*** *(This) does not prohibit or limit any effort by an institution of higher education to encourage and recruit qualified women and minorities to seek admission to such institution* ***if such recruitment or en-***

> ***couragement does not involve granting preferential treatment, in selecting any person for admission, that is based in whole or in part on race, sex, color, ethnicity, or national origin.***[xliv]

Fortunately, this amendment did not pass. Yet, you can see its potential damage. It would have eliminated opportunity for many of our people across the board, a la Clarence Thomas. Now, ask yourself this very serious question—Did you hear about this before today?

We live during a time where states' rights are returning to prominence. A century ago, states' rights produced the Civil War and Jim Crow. It appears that the pendulum is swinging back to bygone days. This is why our witness as Christians must shape discussions and awareness about "the least of these." A biblical history of standing up against injustice, from figures such as Moses and Esther, encourage our holy boldness. Many of us are direct beneficiaries of this type of witness. We must do our part in using all the tools at our disposal, whether they be voting or personal and collective industry, to make a difference. We then leave the part we can't do ourselves to God. And I believe God's record is one we can trust.

A View on Suffering
March 20, 2011

On March 11, an earthquake took place off of the coast of Japan, and as a result a tsunami devastated cities in the northern part of that country. It was the most powerful earthquake ever to hit this land, and over 10,000 people have died as of this writing. In addition to the cleanup and recovery efforts, Japan faces the worst nuclear emergency since Chernobyl.

As we view this horrific scene, some commentary comes to the surface. Many point an accusatory finger at God, feeling that God is unfair and has abdicated responsibility. This causes others to question God's existence. In his book, *The Reason for God*, Timothy Keller cites that suffering proves a better argument for God's existence than one against it. [xlv]

How?

We see suffering and its challenges through the natural order of the world's ebb and flow. Life, for example, is marvelous for a lion and challenging for a wildebeest. Our problems with suffering and who and how it hits actually says more about us than it does about God, for it is our attempt to place our private morality on a universe that is truly beyond our comprehension—or as our president once said, "beyond [our] pay grade." The Christian faith never fully answers the "why" of suffering; I submit that the full answer would overwhelm us. We do, however, have the assurance that in our suffering God shows up and is with us.

We have the supreme example in Jesus, who left the lush economy and location of heaven for the mundane reality of this world, coming into the midst of human suffering. On the cross, Jesus endured temporary separation from the Father, due to the sacrifice He bore for the world. He suffered the anguish of separation and violation that He didn't merit or earn, yet He withstood.

God, relating to humanity's sense of loss at what happened in Japan, now equips those directly affected by the tragedy and us with resilience and camaraderie to face this important hour.

Where to Put Burdens in the Midst of Confusion
October 20, 2002

We live during one of the most unsettled times in recent history. With the collapse of the Berlin Wall and the dismantling of the Soviet Union, many perceived that the world was finally at peace, and the moral laxity that we saw was the only challenge to our way of life. Today we know differently. The sense of peace and security that once accompanied us in buildings and other public places are nonexistent. Terrorists are in dark corners waiting for new opportunities to create mayhem. Many of us foresee the eventual dysfunction of the Social Security system, but we didn't expect the present shakiness of many 401(k) and other pension plans. The stock market, which once was a symbol of a soaring eagle, is now an example of the latest amusement park rollercoaster ride.

When we couple the national and international scene with local realities, the scenario remains the same. Our own personal challenges and conflicts add an extra nervous energy. Life in this century has a more frantic and fearsome pace than ever before. Consider this—the cave man merely hunted and fished, but the modern man deals with the upkeep of his home, the safety of his family, the hectic pace of his commute, the politics of his office, the paucity of his paycheck, and the protection of his meager assets. The mental stress of it all is causing many to pass away before their time. The common denominator of all of this is worry. Unsettled events, whether national, societal or personal, create worry. Worry creates the treadmill we know as stress.

Jesus has a personal answer for where we find ourselves. It is personal because it is forged in our relationship with Him. Plainly speaking, if we have no relationship with Jesus, the following cannot apply to us: *Come to me, all you who are weary and burdened, and I will give you rest. Take my yoke upon you and learn from me, for I am gentle and humble in heart, and you will find rest for your souls. For my yoke is easy and my burden is light* (Matthew 11:28-30). There are times when we will get tired, burnt out and overwhelmed. When this happens, Jesus waits with outstretched arms of love, ready to take our burdens from us. Jesus is our anchor for our past and present, and our security for our future. He is our certain hope. Therefore, let us take our uncertainties and fears to Him. After all, He has asked for them!

Watchfulness in Uncertain Times
February 2, 2003

We stand on the brink of war. Eloquent words and pithy phrases would only cloud this basic fact. Every day soldiers are being sent to the Persian Gulf and South Korea. Our conversations have shifted from "if" to "when." President Bush, in his State of the Union address on Tuesday, sharpened the war sword as he talked about Saddam Hussein and his Iraqi regime.

In times like these, many people wish to find a place of escape from conversations of war. The church, for some, is that place. In times like these, however, we can't take an ostrich's view of life and put our heads in the sand. Being, as Jesus described, *the salt of the earth* (Matthew 5:13), we must know what is happening around us so we can properly season the world. We must also know so we, like the men of Issachar, can understand the times. It is safe to say that no one in this country disagrees that Saddam Hussein is guilty of heinous acts. The difference of opinion is in how to deal with this problem. We are being geared toward war because of what *could* happen, instead of what has been done. Iraq is a threat, but up until today it has not been proven that it has attacked the sovereignty of our nation. To attack Iraq's sovereignty without any "smoking gun" is equal to whipping a child who has been wayward in the past because we believe the child is thinking about doing wrong in the near future.

Something ought to be done about the challenges to world peace in Iraq and North Korea. These challenges can be met with something other than war. Impoverished North Korea is being courted by the possibility of financial aid instead of violence. Alternative means—other than financial aid—can be applied to Iraq as well. Remember, at one time both Saddam and Osama bin Laden were our allies when it suited our purposes. One of the root causes of where we are today stems from the desire of others to access our standard of living. Unable to gain entry, they then attempt to dismantle it. This analysis does not absolve them of guilt; it merely points out that the Christian principle of being concerned about the least of these should always be at the forefront of what we do. Many would say that we are a Christian nation—in spite of slavery, genocide of the Native Americans, and economic, environmental and societal racism. It is now time, through our collective actions, to prove it.

As we walk into uncertain times let us pray so that we receive a "Hezekiah moment." In 2 Kings 20:1-5 the prophet Isaiah told Hezekiah, *This is what the LORD says: Put your house in order, because you are going to die; you will not recover." Hezekiah turned his face to the wall and prayed to the LORD, "Remember, O LORD, how I have walked before you faithfully and with wholehearted devotion and have done what is good in your eyes." And Hezekiah wept bitterly. Before Isaiah had left the middle court, the word of the LORD came to him: "Go back and tell Hezekiah, the leader of my people, `This is what the LORD, the God of your father David, says: I have heard your prayer and seen your tears; I will heal you. On the third day from now you will go up to the temple of the LORD.* Perhaps if the righteous pray, God will deliver us from this perilous situation; if He does not, we already have the assurance that we can rest in our relationship with Him.

God [is] our refuge and strength, a very present help in trouble. Therefore will not we fear, though the earth be removed, and though the mountains be carried into the midst of the sea (Psalm 46:1-2 KJV).

An Example of the Power of God
March 16, 2003

On this day two weeks ago, one of our members was presented with impossible odds. Physicians met with her family and shared with them the bleak nature of their loved one's situation. The words that were presented were overwhelmingly pessimistic; they had the force of heavy sledgehammers. After all, doctors are trained in this work and know what they see. For this family, Sunday night was like the night before Easter Sunday for the followers of Jesus; for whom it seemed that the best thing to do was to rise early the next morning, Sunday, and prepare Jesus' body for proper burial.

There is someone reading this who has received a disrespectful slap from life. Someone who can adequately and accurately assess your life has told you that your existence can get no better. You have been living in the midnight before Easter for a long time. Now you face the challenge of dealing with your situation head on.

Monday morning came for the family and their loved one. Something happened. An eight hour procedure took four hours. A four hour recovery time took two. And so far, all of the pessimistic forecasts have not materialized. A miracle has taken place. Many of you have seen this miracle person, and have seen for yourself the awesome power of God.

God is moving in our midst, and God is not through. Lent is a time of reflection, and we should now begin to listen, and watch all of the ways that God is trying to get our attention. God wants to change the circumstances of your life, and draw you closer. Our challenges—whether personal, family, or as a church—are opportunities for God to show us His power, presence, majesty, and might. Realize that as a Christian, you are firmly planted in the resurrection. Therefore, our circumstances are not finally decided by what we see, but by who God is.

A Bad Number
December 18, 2016

220. As of right now.

Murders, that is.

As we begin to celebrate the Christmas season at First Baptist with the 76th rendition of Handel's *Messiah*, we can't forget the context for our ministry—Memphis, Tennessee. As the current mayor is "mad as hell" about the above number, and as a former mayor tells us it's a "black problem," we still die. And today, as we celebrate this season, at 6:00 p.m. one of the chairs in our orchestra will be empty. Chris Waters, one of our musicians for the past few years, was murdered during a home invasion. He is now one among the number of those whose lives didn't just pass, but were taken.

This reminds us that the Church will never be obsolete or go out of business. Why? Because at the lowest common denominator, we battle spiritual issues anchored in sin. As you read this, many of you equate this with reclamation of the individual. Part of the remedy is anchored in a relationship with Jesus Christ, which should change both a life and its character for the better. However, we must also address the sinfulness of unjust systems created by unjust people, which create an environment that is a cauldron of crime and unrest. The primary targets and perpetrators of these murders—young black males—didn't happen in a vacuum or because young black men are more criminal. Many of these same people make up the third of black men in this county without citizenship rights.

As we celebrate Jesus today, let's remember that while He came for the individual, He also came to tear down unjust systems. Until we address the second part of this equation with as much relish as the first, we will continue to spin out of control.

220. As of right now…

Hang in There — God is With You
May 15, 2016

Let us not become weary in doing good, for at the proper time we will reap a harvest if we do not give up. Therefore, as we have opportunity, let us do good to all people, especially to those who belong to the family of believers (Galatians 6:9-10).

If any of us would venture to be candid, all of us at times get weary. Sometimes it's caused by the enormity of our lives, for it seems that waves of challenges come our way similar to waves crashing on the shore. A second reason could be the need for rest. A greater reason, I think, is due to a general sense of disillusionment. The reality of life is simply that most people like you because of what they think you can do for them, or who they may think or know you are. Others may feel threatened, but do the nice/nasty routine, sort of like what the O'Jays sang about in their song "Backstabbers." You know the lyric, "They smile in your face; all the time they want to take your place…" These things happen to all of us, and could make us discouraged.

Because of the prospect of being weary, we feel the pregnant urge to give up. The temptation to yield to the comfort of convenience confronts us. I had a recent season of this type of weariness, and as I sat still and pondered this, the verses of Scripture you see above planted themselves in my mind. What these verses imply is you can continue to do good to those around you if you recalibrate your focus. It's really not about how others see and appreciate you, it's about being faithful to what God has entrusted you to do. In other words, God pays attention, and we will reap the fruits of our labor at the right time.

You never fully know when the reaping will take place, but it doesn't matter, God will sustain you; and when you trust God, your strength will be renewed.

The Ruler of Oceans, Stars and Sky
March 15, 2015

As you remember, we recently had an unusual batch of weather for the month of March, when about 5 inches of snow made landfall here in the normally temperate winter climate of Memphis. Schools closed, supermarkets sold out of eggs and bread, Bible studies and worship took place at home instead with a church family, and a new generation of children acquainted themselves with sledding and building a snowman for the first time.

As I prepared for our Thursday morning prayer conference call, a thought hit me: *Is there a way to stop or prevent snow?* I decided to use the 21st century's limited but quick operating replacement for the Encyclopedia Britannica of my youth—the internet search engine. I typed in this important question to see what it would yield. As I read through the results, I found some interesting responses. Many of them dealt with either snow removal or dressing for the weather. Only one response dealt with the prevention of snow; it was a "good witch" webpage that had a spell for banishing even the appearance of snow. I guess they are the modern-day descendants of the Baal prophets in 1 Kings 17:26-29. They had the same results as their ancestors, for as you know, it did snow, and continues to do so all over the world.

I realize you already knew the answer to my question. Resorts in various areas can seed clouds to create snow, but there is no invention to prevent it. That is the sole providence of God. In an era where scientific and technological advancements make what used to be miraculous mundane and common, we sometimes lose the awe and majesty toward the One who can do and see beyond anything we could ever ask or think of. The basic human reality remains the same – even at our best, we have limitations to what and whom we can control. We must rely on Someone who is greater than us.

The good thing about this reliance is that because of our relationship with Him, God cares for us. God wants the best for us, even when we can't see what that may be. And when it does snow, God will never leave us or forsake us. Eventually, in the midst of God's presence, the snow in our lives will melt away, while God's presence remains. What a comforting thought and reality.

CHAPTER TEN - FAMILY MATTERS & PERSONAL REFLECTIONS AS I SEE IT

The Great Role of the Elders
May 19, 1996

Today we celebrate Senior Citizens Day. We remember the contributions of those who have led the way by stamina and strength for many years, and who now lead by watchfulness and wisdom. Many pertinent sayings of sage mother wit have been passed down through the ages, such as "Every tub must sit on its own bottom," "If you don't have the best of everything, make the best of everything you have," "Keeping up with the Joneses will keep you down," and "A robin's song ain't pretty to a worm." We are indeed blessed by the witness of the seniors in our ranks. Many of us who are younger owe much to our seniors. A famous comedian once said "You have a lot of people who call old folks fools, but there are a lot of young dead geniuses." As Dr. King once said, "Longevity has its place."

Our text for today highlights Caleb, and how he continued to set an example for the Israelites into his eighty-fifth year. Out of his testimony about the Promised Land, Joshua led the Israelites into Canaan. Both Caleb and Joshua were elder statesmen among the Jews at this time, for all Israelites over forty years old, except for these two men, had died in the wilderness. Caleb continued to lead by his willingness to conquer new territory.

My prayer is that those of you among us who are seniors will possess the spirit of Caleb. Perhaps your strength has ebbed, but you still possess an abundance of wisdom. Your footsteps may be slow, but your prayers are as fast as ever.

Our church faces new and unique challenges ahead; you among us who are seniors are definitely a part of that future. God has allowed you see the great past of First Baptist; your willingness and wisdom are required and necessary to help First Baptist see what lies ahead for us in a clearer way. Let us continue to build on the past, and strive toward the future.

Pray for Your Pastor
December 17, 2000

Over the past few weeks, I've begun a personal, customary process for this time of year. I evaluate my personal and ministerial development. The instruments I use aren't based on any person's positive or negative opinions. My benchmarks are developed based on Scripture. I also attempt to periodically review the role of a pastor and a Christian from a theological and a societal point of view.

As I pondered where I am at the present, I viewed the societal changes to the role of pastor. In the past, the role of pastor was mainly a priestly one. Pastors practiced the "ministry of presence;" they led worship, preached, and provided a listening ear. As the church developed, other pieces were added to this role. The reality of good business practices gave the pastor administrative responsibilities. Developing willing and equipped volunteers added the necessity of leadership development. The complex needs of a congregation connected to an ethnic culture (i.e., African-American) dictated the need for a holistic social ministry to address the challenges of a community.

If you think about it, I've just described an impossible job. Many pastors face unbelievable stress, burnout, and sometimes depression. However, the task of Christ-centered ministry is completed in churches all over the world, including our own. Why? Because the power to complete the task is not found in us, but in God. God allows us to participate in this process through both our Christian witness and prayer. Prayer is the essential oil needed to make the machinery of the church and our lives run properly.

I ask you today to pray for me; that God would make me the pastor and leader I should be and will become. And I will continue to pray for you; that God will develop, sustain and prosper you to His glory. By praying and working together, I firmly believe that the best days of First Baptist are yet to come.

The Importance of Family
January 12, 2003

This past Thursday I was in Queens, New York at the funeral of my cousin, Mrs. Cynthia Taylor. I had the unique privilege and responsibility of delivering the "Pastor's Message." My experience is mentioned in this space because all of us at some point will sit in the seat of the bereaved. Several of you over the last few weeks have experienced this firsthand. The Bible puts it this way in Psalm 90:10, *The length of our days is seventy years – or eighty, if we have the strength; yet their span is but trouble and sorrow, for they quickly pass, and we fly away.*

Out of this experience, clear focus is brought to several realities that shape life. During these times we are reminded of the importance of family. It seems to always take a funeral, especially of certain family members, to pull family together. Given that human nature is what it is, we usually cease to gather except in times of crisis. Wednesday night I met many family members for the first time, and found out about the present roots of the Hutchinson clan; with branches in England, Canada, Cuba, the Cayman Islands, Jamaica, Malaysia, and the United States. Many of you have had similar experiences in meeting family. We must remember that during times of challenge our family is our bedrock of support. Regardless of circumstances or disagreements, we must remember our love for and connection with each other. The same dynamic applies to our church family. United we hold up the banner of our Christian witness to the world, and stand with each other during good and challenging times.

During our bereavement, we are reminded of the need for and the role of God in the midst of life. Personal achievements, while important, take a back seat when a challenge such as illness comes. Sitting at the gravesite reminds us in many ways that we are truly aliens in a sorrow filled land called life; and the grand, glorious vistas of eternal life for those who know Jesus await. We are able to see, for example, when we read an obituary how God's hand was active during the course of a well lived life. These times also remind us how God blesses families in the midst of their growth. I observed Thursday how our family, with active roots as involved laypersons in the Episcopal church, has now spread out over five denominations, the constant being faith in Jesus Christ.

I pray that all of us, if we have not done so already, will begin to strengthen the bonds of family and faith. Let us not wait, for the loved one you plan to meet tomorrow may leave this world today, and the opportunity you have for salvation by grace expires at death.

What a Fellowship
July 6, 2003

This past Sunday at 3:00 pm, history was made. The oldest African-American Baptist church originally organized in the city of Memphis, and the mother church of the Church of God in Christ got together to praise the Lord. Temple COGIC graciously invited us as special guests for their Family and Friends Day. There is a running joke that the only time our two churches meet is in the funeral home that physically separates us. As of last Sunday, this is no longer the case. In fact, Pastor Hall and the Temple family gave us a beautiful plaque to commemorate the occasion. It will now stand as tangible proof that we have fellowshipped together before our transport to heaven.

There are reasons why this hasn't taken place until now. The Church of God in Christ is a denomination that was birthed out of the Baptist church and the Azusa Street charismatic movement of the early 20th century. Because of this history, there are only two major differences between "them" and "us". One is their emphasis on the gifts of the spirit; the second is the style of worship. Neither of these constitutes grave doctrinal error on their part or ours, just differences in interpretation. Despite doctrinal differences and differences in style, we are all Christians. We as the Church have sometimes taken on a more separatist attitude than those in the world, focusing on what divides us rather than on the great work that God commissioned for our hands.

The best way I can think of to illustrate this point is from a page from my own life's story. In 1993, around this time of year, I was in Kenya. As our group left the capital city of Nairobi on our way to Amboseli National Park, we were told not to take pictures of Maasai warriors without their permission. These warriors have a fierce, well-earned reputation throughout East Africa as people you want to keep as friends, not enemies. Many times in the past, Maasai have been exploited, with their pictures earning money for the photographers, but not the subjects. After receiving this information, I found myself in the wilderness hours later, in a minivan with teenage boys. We had just passed three young Maasai warriors about 20 yards down the road when our minivan got a flat. Cameras suddenly went under the seats and we got off the bus so we could change the tire. When we stepped off the bus, we found ourselves face to face with the same warriors we just passed on the side of the road, and they did not look happy to see us. They were fully armed, with 7-foot long spears that had 3-foot long blades. As you can imagine, the temperature of our prayer lives increased immediately.

The Kenyan driver, who told us about the warriors and who was not Maasai, nervously began to change the tire. Our youth stood off to the side, and the warriors stood within arms-length of them. I was busy helping the driver—because faith without works is dead—and twirled the tire iron on the lug nuts to speed up the process. This caused the warriors to chuckle and broke the ice. At this point we get to the part of the story that has direct application to last Sunday. Our young men then felt at ease and began to whisper among themselves about the appearance of the warriors. The Maasai were wearing their standard warrior uniforms—finely braided hair dyed with henna for a slightly reddish tint, maroon cloth that served as a long tunic, and their spears. Our young men pointed in amazement at the haberdashery of the Maasai and chuckled with admiration and awe. They wore the standard clothing of circa 1993 youth—FUBU shirts, baggy jeans, and baseball caps; Air Jordan, Air Force One and Reebok sneakers. The warriors pointed in amazement at the haberdashery of our young men and chuckled with admiration and awe. When the spare tire was on, all of us shook hands, and waved good-bye as we went our separate ways. Aunt Hagar's children, those rooted from Africa but living in New York and those still "at home" in Kenya, were able, for a few brief moments, to marvel over their differences yet come together for meaningful fellowship.

I pray that there will be other times where we will put down our differences for a few moments, remembering that we have the same Creator and Brother, and praise the Lord together.

I'm Not Supposed to be Here
January 3, 2010

According to medical science, I'm not supposed to be here. As I reflect on having another birthday, a true story comes to mind once again. Over 50 years ago Agnes Hutchinson, a nurse, wanted to have a child. Her biological clock shouted for attention, and a visit to the doctor turned into surgery and then the proclamation that pregnancy would never take place. Heartbroken, she decided to lean on the reservoir of faith that had brought her to that point in her life, and she discussed her situation with God. This hurting woman remembered the prayer of Hannah in the Old Testament. She asked God to give her a healthy child with ten fingers and ten toes, and in turn, she would make sure that the child grew to love and know God.

One day, she noticed a change in her body, and returned to the doctor. Based on her medical experience, she shared with the doctor her belief that she was pregnant. The doctor, based on his experience, told Mrs. Hutchinson that she was hoping against hope. In fact, the doctor believed that this hunch on the part of his patient came from the failure of the previous procedure to correct her problem, and, because of this, recommended additional surgery. Many people at this point would have followed medical advice, but something in this patient caused her to remember her conversation with God, and she held her course. Forty-nine years ago, God answered her prayer when I was born. Time won't permit me to share all of the wonderful things I've been able to see and do during my eventful lifetime, or the great people I've met, including you. And just like Samuel, today I do what I do because of the providential hand of God.

Many of you are not supposed to be here. Think of all the blessings you've received, the battles you've won, and the challenges you've overcome that were supposed to be failures, but God said otherwise. Many times so-called experts are wrong. According to them, Black Americans should still be drinking from fountains labeled "Colored," living only in one section of town, and never seeing a Black president. We should all be glad that God supersedes pundits.

So in this New Year, grab hold of the impossible by faith. Live the impossible dream. Be successful in what "you're not supposed to do." I'm a living witness that God will see you through.

A Look at Domestic Violence
October 18, 2015

Domestic Violence Sunday is being observed in many churches around Memphis today. It's a subject that we in the church tend to avoid, trying to grab the sanctimonious broom to sweep it under the rug. Yet if we're truthful, we know several victims of this violence—from women and men to abused children, and even elders taken advantage of by their own family and acquaintances. The reality is that this ostrich can still be seen; for even though its head is in the proverbial sand, its tail is exposed.

The purpose of this uncomfortable conversation is multi-faceted. First, we must, as alluded to earlier, acknowledge the existence of domestic violence. The starting place for addressing this scourge is to bring it to light.

Second, we must understand the wounds and dysfunction it's caused in our midst. Some conflicts and challenges we have in dealing with each other often have nothing to do with how we love Jesus but are due to unresolved trauma in our past. We then find an unwitting soul to pay the cost of someone else's transgressions, yet the problem isn't fixed.

Third, we must know that healing and deliverance from these situations can happen. Enclosed in your *Herald* is information on how you can get help. Thanks to UAV 901, the group that sponsored both the March Against Violence and the letter to the Shelby County DA, we have a brochure that includes a prayer guide along with both "Where to go" and "How can I help" information cards. We will also keep some in the church. And remember, you can always call me.

Lastly, it isn't God's desire that you endure this type of trauma or exist with unresolved hurt that handcuffs your life. I pray that this discussion creates a climate of helpfulness, sensitivity and deliverance in our midst.

For those still unconvinced that it's necessary for today's church to address this subject, consider these facts:

- Every nine seconds in the United States, a woman is assaulted or beaten.
- On average, nearly 20 people per minute are physically abused by an intimate partner in the United States. During one year, this equates to more than 10 million women and men.
- 1 in 3 women and 1 in 4 men have been victims of [some form of] physical violence by an intimate partner within their lifetime.
- 1 in 5 women and 1 in 7 men have been victims of severe physical violence by an intimate partner in their lifetime.
- 1 in 7 women and 1 in 18 men have been stalked by an intimate partner during their lifetime to the point where they felt very fearful or believed that they or someone close to them would be harmed or killed.
- On a typical day, there are more than 20,000 phone calls placed to domestic violence hotlines nationwide.[xlvi]

Based on these numbers, you know someone or are sitting next to someone or are someone who has been through, or is going through, this fire. The comforting thing to know is that God has healing with your name on it. I pray that today is the beginning of that healing for some, and the needed continuation for others.

Decisions Have Consequences
June 6, 2017

Go back in your memory with me, to how you were instructed to tackle life's repetitive moments. Remember the first time you were shown how to boil an egg, or how to run your own bathwater, or how to clean. Later, you may have learned how to cook, and then how to drive. In all of these activities, you relieved your parent(s) of some responsibility when you became proficient in what you were taught. However, the real point was training you for the future.

Many a decision made in the present has ramifications for the future. A national electorate, wooed by promises anchored in ether, now watches testimony from a former FBI director who worked with both a Republican and Democratic president. He trusted both of them but took notes during meetings with the current one because of trust issues. He saw through the ether because he understood a basic tenet he undoubtedly learned during his youth—truthfulness.

We often talk about what our youth don't do, what they won't do, and what they don't understand. What we miss is that whatever they know or don't know is our responsibility. A young life isn't preformed. Across the board, for most living creatures, some nurturing must take place to prepare the young for adulthood. This past week we had our Vacation Bible School, where we taught youth from the cradle roll through high school about Jesus. By faith, we "train up a child" and trust that God will work through our efforts.

The labor is constant, the training can be intense or spotty, but the potential payoff is not only great, but impacts a community. When a young person develops into an adult who continues the circle of life, we are all the better. And it all starts from learning how to boil an egg…and learning about Jesus.

CHAPTER ELEVEN - EMPOWERMENT 101

We Can Make It with the Lord and Each Other
July 9, 1995

As we gather in corporate worship on this day, we should review the events that are currently challenging our nation. The Southern Baptists apologized last week for their part in the very institution which was instrumental in their formation – slavery. Last Thursday, the Supreme Court ruled that using race as a "predominant factor" in drawing Congressional district lines is unconstitutional. This comes after a previous ruling by this same court, in which affirmative action in governmental bids was challenged. Ironically, Clarence Thomas, a primary beneficiary of affirmative action, wrote the majority opinion. All these events have taken place while we watch our people continuously self-destruct. We continue to kill each other because Black life is cheap. Nathan McCall, in his autobiography, *Makes Me Wanna Holler*, recounts how he received thirty days in jail for almost killing a Black man, and twelve years for robbing a McDonald's restaurant.[xlvii]

In order to move forward, we must go back to the bridges that brought us over. As I have said in different ways, **we**, along with the Lord, will determine our survival. One of the reasons we are not (collectively) doing a good job arises out of our overwhelming acceptance of cultural norms. We want the American Dream **now!** Because of this, our people, for the most part denied the economic power to bring this to pass, scramble to achieve a goal that is out of reach. Those of us with a closer reach forsake family and friends in this race; those with a distant reach resort to drive-by shootings and destructive behavior. Our experience as Christians and African-Americans should remind us to place our focus on the Lord, and each other. We must demonstrate our love for Christ out of our love for each other. Our foreparents did this, and we stand today able to reap the benefits of their wisdom.

We can continue to be excited about our relationship with the Lord, knowing that in our faithfulness the Lord will see us through. Our excitement will enable our brothers and sisters to change their focus from the material and mundane to the eternal and excellent.

We Must Support Our Own
October 28, 1995

This past week, I had the opportunity to attend banquets given by the UNCF and the Urban League. These banquets were well conceived and put together, and prominent people from across the city were in attendance. Their presence gave the hosts a chance, especially in the case of the Urban League, to stress the plight and fiscal condition of their organizations.

What is to be made of this? If we are honest, every tangible organization in our community, outside of the church, is supported and kept alive by businesses and benefactors outside of our community. Many of them have seen the need for diversity in the workplace, and the support of institutions assisting with this goal. Our current tax laws presently reward individuals and corporations for their altruism. However, the tide is beginning to shift. Some are beginning to push the idea of a flat tax, which would do away with charitable contributions as a deduction. Many individuals, corporations, and institutions are tiring from the burden of carrying non-profit organizations.

This space has been intentionally used in the past in focus on self-empowerment. In only one instance, in regard to a downtown school, has the subject of race relations been discussed even in a tangential way in this space. God goes beyond our pigmentation to the condition of our heart; and so must we. However, I believe that we also must concentrate on self advancement and empowerment. We must, to paraphrase Scripture, deal with the problems in our own eye before we deal with the problems elsewhere.

The organizations in our community are meeting places for the races, where we can begin to shatter preconceived notions about one another. However, they are also training grounds where many of our people can be prepared for the 21st century.

I write these words today because I am grateful for the assistance of others. They have cared for some of the issues in our community in a tangible way. However, I also clearly see that the window of opportunity is slowly beginning to close. Those of us who have been blessed by God with tangible wherewithal must, right now, make a lifelong commitment to the infrastructure of our community. In this work, we must always remember that through the power of Christ and our relationship with Him, this will be possible. Countless generations are depending on us.

Legacy and Responsibility
February 4, 1998

Today begins another celebration of Black History Month. We look over the rich legacy that we as a people have had during four centuries on this continent. Our people have contributed to the economic, social and spiritual well being of this nation from its inception. From the traffic light to the lawnmower, the filament for the light bulb to the oil filter, the refrigerator to the mailbox, the golf tee to "the real McCoy", we have made a lasting contribution.

Our sermon for this morning looks at a tension point between some of our people and the Church. Our text, found in Genesis 9, has been used to legitimize the subjugation of our people. Some, looking back over this abuse, have unjustly tagged the responsibility for this act on the Church universally, instead of on those misguided and hateful individuals. It is my hope that this sermon will add to a better understanding of this abuse, and add a healthy way to view it. When viewing the text, two things become clear. The so-called curse of Ham didn't take place, for Canaan was the specific subject of Noah's wrath. His ethnicity wasn't a factor, especially when several scholars tell us that all of the people in this story had the same African-based bloodlines. Essentially, it was more a case of a grandfather saying that a grandson would turn out like his "no good" daddy.

For some of you, this issue may not be an important one. You have conquered it, and moved on to "weightier" matters. Recognize, however, that many of our people continue to live in psychological bondage due to this issue; it is one that is subconsciously believed by many of our people. The nonsensical violence that continuously creates premature funerals for our youth testify to this reality. As the editorial in this week's *Memphis Flyer* indicates, this city is a hazardous place if you are African-American. The issue of self-image must be addressed if we are to proceed as a collective body.

Finally, in all of this discussion there is hope. It is a hope resident in a God who took us from the bowels of slavery, who helped us create a new life in the air of freedom, and who remains with us today. We have hope today, in spite of Newt Gingrich or the National Affairs Briefing held recently here in Memphis at the Pyramid, because of Jesus Christ. This month should remind us, above all else, that *…greater is He that is in you, than he who is in the world* (1 John 4:4 KJV).

How Strong Is Our Money?
November 15, 1998

One week ago Saturday, a group of about fifteen First Baptist members went to see the movie *Beloved.* This movie deals with, among other things, the psychological impact of slavery. Our group was supposed to see this movie at the Southbrook Cinema, the only African-American owned movie theater in the state of Tennessee. However, at the last minute we were unable to do so. The film, slated to stay at the Cinema until Thanksgiving, was pulled by the movie studio.

Southbrook Cinema, in the heart of Whitehaven, is one of the few theaters located within a reasonable proximity to a large segment of African-Americans. In spite of this, *Beloved*, with its focus, was initially targeted away from Southbrook Cinema. Only after an intense public campaign did the movie studio relent and allow Southbrook to show the movie during its initial offering. *Beloved* continues to run in several other theaters, most of them a long country drive from where many of our people live.

This discussion, at least on the surface level, is not about racism. Too often we focus on race at the neglect of other important issues. Many of us remember the time when a movie like *Beloved* would not be made. Since then, African-American images have become commonplace on the movie screen, although there is room for greater exposure. The bottom line of this particular discussion is money. This movie was undoubtedly yanked from Southbrook Cinema because it was not pulling in the necessary revenue.

The strength of the African-American business community is important as we enter the 21st century. A strong business is the engine that affects quality-of-life issues. For example, the Memphis business community—especially the real estate, tourism and construction industries—is the driving force behind the downtown renaissance. Money also brings equality. What changed the mind of the Montgomery Bus Company, for example, was declining revenue, not its "love" for our people.

One of the ways we can help to strengthen our communities is to support our businesses. In several cases this will involve sacrifice. I would imagine that many of the newer movie theaters, for example, have levels of ambiance that Southbrook Cinema at this time cannot imitate. In seeing this instance in light of supporting businesses in our communities collectively, we must decide, as the writer of Hebrews 11 tells us of Moses in verse 25, *to suffer affliction with the people of God, than to enjoy the pleasures of sin for a season* (KJV).

You Can Begin to Lead from Where You Are
July 18, 1999

This past week I happened to see some of the new Chris Rock comedy special. Despite his vulgar use of the King's English, he made some interesting observations; two of which had an immediate impact on me. In the first monologue, Rock talked about school violence in the wake of Columbine. He then shifted into the abilities of parents raising children. He quipped, "What do you mean you can't tell if a child's gonna be successful? Here's a clue: If he calls his grandmother "Ma," and his mother "Pam," he's on his way to jail. You won't be saving tuition money; you'll be saving bail money." His second observation involved leadership. Rock said that African-Americans need a leader. According to him, we haven't had a real leader since Dr. Martin Luther King, Jr. He then added that he wants a leader that can "move" him.

Rock's view on leadership is one held by many in our community. However, practical wisdom and changing times dictate that the time of one mass leader has probably gone the way of the 8-track tape deck. Just from casual observation in our communities, we can probably agree that it is the "best of times and the worst of times." Good leadership is vital if progression is to be made into the 21st century.

Through the witness of Scripture, we hear these words in 1 Peter 2, verses 5 and 9*: you also, like living stones, are being built into a spiritual house to be a holy priesthood, offering spiritual sacrifices acceptable to God through Jesus Christ…But you are a chosen people, a royal priesthood, a holy nation, a people belonging to*

God, that you may declare the praises of him who called you out of darkness into his wonderful light. In plain language, each of us, in our own way, are called upon to be leaders. We have more influence than we could ever imagine, and our individual leadership is an untapped resource in the midst of our families and communities.

Toward the end of Acts, Paul and Silas were greeted with persecution from several quarters. The Judiazers, who were those living a legalistic type of Christianity, and the Gentiles who were hearing the gospel for the first time presented to these men a constant challenge. In Acts 17:6, several of these people dragged some believers before the city officials, shouting, *These men who have caused trouble all over the world have now come here.* It was an exclamation of trouble, but it was also an acknowledgement of Paul's influence.

Many of you are quite active in the Memphis community. If there were no First Baptist, Memphis would be in a severely challenged condition, to say the least. Allow me to end our conversation today with these words; if you are not making a positive difference in any way, start today. If you are, encourage others to follow your great example. In doing so, you will continue the legacy of First Baptist as it "witnesses for God in the Crossroads of the Mid-South."

What You Can Do
May 5, 2002

The hiring of Jerry West by the Memphis Grizzlies this past week was a landmark event in the history of this city. It isn't notable solely because of what it will do for the basketball franchise, which will be significant; nor is it notable because of Mr. West's residency in our city. Many of the issues that we have as a city will continue to be present alongside Mr. West and his presence in Memphis. The importance is anchored in what it means for the psyche of this city. Geoff Calkins, a columnist for the *Commercial Appeal*, put it best in his piece on May 1, 2002 titled, "Nothing Memphis Can't Do." He writes, "All things are possible in this city. All things. Don't scoff. There is no longer a built-in excuse for failing to think big. Can't happen in Memphis? Don't give me that... Don't listen to the wise guys. Don't listen to those who would tell you this is Memphis, so it can't possibly be done. Kemmons Wilson didn't listen. Neither did Fred Smith… We're too small, too muggy, too inept? Don't bring that weak stuff in here. It can happen in Memphis. All it takes is energy, a vision and unmitigated gall."[xlviii]

The ability to have faith in the impossible did not start with a town and a basketball team. It began with a man who at 70 years old believed a God who told him to leave his home but gave him no roadmap. God then considered this man righteous because of his faith. It continued through the Old Testament to the New, where the disciples of Jesus were presented with a difficult situation. A demon-possessed boy was brought to them for healing, but they could not do it. Why not? Hear Jesus' explanation: *Because* *you have so little faith. I tell you the truth, if you have faith as small as a mustard seed, you can say to this mountain, `Move from here to there' and it will move. Nothing will be impossible for you.* (Matthew 17:20 ESV)

We can't always see how to meet life's challenges. We can't always see how to cause great things to happen in our church, our places of employment, or our personal lives. Jesus' response to His disciples encourages us to look past circumstances in faith to Him. He is also letting us know that if the flame of our faith lamp is low—the size of a mustard seed—it is still enough to do great things. This reality is captured in this particular verse in God's Word: *I can do all things through Christ which strengtheneth me.* (Philippians 4:13 KJV)

The Real Fix for an Entrenched Problem
February 16, 2003

After weeks of on and off discussion about the impending war against Iraq, it was my intent this week to place an inspirational nugget in this space. However, the local events of this week—during Black History Month—prevent me from doing so. On Monday afternoon a Trezevant student was forcibly moved from the land of the living by gunfire initiated by one of his peers—a 15 year-old. That same day, an 88-year-old retired science teacher was mugged in the parking lot of a store. The robber grabbed her purse, and, during the struggle, the senior woman fell backward, hit her head and was knocked unconscious. She died the next day.

These events, unfortunately, are also part of Black History. When you add them to all of the despicable drive-by shootings, self-demeaning behavior and senseless killings, they chronicle the self-destruction of a people. Historians and sociologists in the years to come will point to this time as one where we had and achieved more, but did less. Recognizing the role of racism, which still exists, it is time to walk away from the familiar adage of "blaming the victim" and do some soul searching. More jails are being built, yet this has not fixed the problem; an increased level of self-awareness through our history constantly takes place, yet this has not fixed the problem either. The death penalty won't fix it because the ones that perform these crimes have a coldness of spirit that won't be deterred or extinguished by death. Complex alarm systems and an armed populace won't work—if a man can create it, another man can break it, and a bullet has no allegiance.

Two things will fix this problem of internal genocide—Jesus and us. Often we forget the true work of the Church. Although we at times provide for those in need, that is only a part of our work. We are in the life transformation business. When Jesus Christ comes into a life, He *transforms* that life. The Bible, in 2 Corinthians 5:17 says, *Therefore, if anyone is in Christ, he is a new creation; the old has gone, the new has come!* After Jesus enters our life, transformation continues. This is known as the pursuit of holiness, or sanctification. It is the act of living the Christian life. Our foreparents described it this way, "Every day with Jesus is sweeter than the day before." A transformed life affects those around it in a positive way. Those who have been transformed have no time to shoot, kill or create mayhem—they are focused on making disciples, and bettering the lot of their peers.

We are the final ingredients in fixing the problem. We are who we are, and where we are, because we were nurtured in the "good ground" of pride in oneself and the knowledge and love of Jesus. Our Sunday school lesson for today highlights the influence that Paul had on Timothy. Timothy, in turn, then had influence on his peers. From our homes to our neighborhoods, let us exude our influence in being the salt of the earth. The perpetrator in the Trezevant student's shooting is up for second degree murder; the perpetrator in the case of the retired teacher is up for first degree murder. Legalities notwithstanding, African-American life will increase in value when we begin to view it as pure gold.

You Can Make a Difference
September 9, 2007

The world seems to abound with evil and confusion. Many people, things and circumstances leave us unhappy, unfulfilled and hurt. Due to these realities, we live in a culture that tells us to increasingly find relief from life's pressures. Relief may be found in illicit recreational activities that give temporary reprieve, doing more harm than good. We are advised to 'let go of the stressors in our lives," but upon further analysis that is not the answer. We may find ourselves living in one neighborhood riddled with challenges, so we run to another only to find the same problems.

It is time that we decide to make a difference where we are. You hold the key to change within your family, your job, your church, and your reality. A saying attributed to philosopher and statesmen Edmund Burke states it plainly: **"The only thing necessary for the triumph of evil is for good men to do nothing."** Indifference is what kills any endeavor. Consider the words of the poet G. A. Studdert Kennedy:

> *When Jesus came to Golgotha they hanged Him on a tree,*
> *They drave great nails through hands and feet, and made a Calvary.*
> *They crowned Him with a crown of thorns, red were His wounds and deep,*
> *For those were crude and cruel days, and human flesh was cheap.*
> *When Jesus came to Birmingham they simply passed Him by,*
> *They never hurt a hair of Him, they only let Him die.*

For men had grown more tender and they would not give Him pain,
They only just passed down the street, and left Him in the rain.[xlix]

Doing nothing is the easiest option, yet the most costly; and is one we can ill afford.

A Symptom and a Solution
November 1, 2009

Last week in Memphis we heard about the young mother who left her two and three year-old sons at home alone while she allegedly ran errands and went shopping. Many people became outraged when the evening news showed an older aunt, a resident of this particular home, callously concerned about getting back in the house to get her purse and its belongings. She showed no regard or care about the welfare of the two children who lived under the same roof.

At the same time in Atlanta, all-male Morehouse College instituted an appropriate attire policy, which includes the banning of wearing women's clothes, hats in buildings, pajamas in public, do-rags, sagging pants, sunglasses in class and walking barefoot on campus. This move, according to those who shaped it, should keep the college firmly in its legacy of shaping outstanding Black men.

How do these two events relate to each other? They are a result of low self-esteem and a lack of proper nurturance; both of which are epidemic in many areas of Black American life today. It seems like common sense to not leave toddlers home alone, yet it was done in the case above with tragic results and is probably more of a common occurrence than we know. And, unfortunately, we see more and more irresponsible aunts like the one in our example. The mother was young, and maybe overwhelmed, but the aunt was seasoned and should have been a better example. It appears that she gave this young mother zero assistance, and was closer to being dead weight. For Morehouse, an institution known for its mandate of shaping great Black leaders, initiating the new dress code is a welcome move.

A symptom is a warning sign, an indicator that something is amiss. We see many indicators, not only in the Black community but across the vast spectrum of American society, that tell us that something is wrong. More often than not, we either close our eyes to it, put a sanctimonious religious veneer on it, or get offended if the "right" person doesn't convey the news in the "right" way. This reaction is similar to that of someone who is having all the obvious signs of a heart attack, yet proceeds with life as usual instead of going to the emergency room.

Changing one's external appearance assists with increasing self-esteem. Looking again at our Morehouse example, we can ask the question, "Would you rather wear shabby clothes or clean, crisp ones?" An attire policy is good, but by itself it can only go so far. However, the ultimate transformation comes from within. The Bible addresses this in several places. Although the ancients never specifically identified self-esteem, its presence is all over Scripture. For instance, Psalm 139:14 reminds us that we are *fearfully and wonderfully made.* Also, the fact that God didn't merely speak but shaped and breathed humankind into existence is evidence that God isn't into junk creation. The beginning of properly adorning the treasure that we are will begin, I believe, the process of valuing lives; both our own and that of others.

The Peace and Prosperity of your City
October 31, 2010

Jeremiah 29:7: *Also, seek the peace and prosperity of the city to which I have carried you into exile. Pray to the LORD for it, because if it prospers, you too will prosper* (NIV).

Our Scripture reference for this conversation is part of a prophetic word given to Jeremiah from God to the Babylonian exiles of the Hebrew Diaspora. They were scattered, and their longing to return to their native soil was so intense that there were some "prophets" who told them they would soon leave Babylon for the familiar surroundings of home. However, God instructed Jeremiah to let the Hebrews know that they should anchor where they were and add to the prosperity and welfare of the city they were in for "if you pray and work for it, it will prosper as you prosper."

This is a practical application to a basic spiritual truth. One's relationship with God should have heavenly wings along with being grounded by earthly feet. Some would point to material gains by the individual as the extent of God's blessings. This thinking is a way of placing the Protestant work ethic behind a sanctimonious, spiritual veneer. The bottom line is God wants us to have a concern about our community; for if it prospers, so do we.

Today the world is in a financial recession. Here in America, small businesses struggle, car dealerships close, credit is tight and jobs disappear. Greed on the part of some places the world in this tough position. Yesterday the voters in Memphis overwhelmingly chose their new mayor. He faces great challenges in pulling this city together, but the responsibility of Memphis isn't his alone. James 2: 15-17 is the New Testament corollary of our text, which reminds us that our faith is demonstrated by works that bless others and meet them at their needs. I agree with Robert McAfee Brown, who in his book, *The Bible Speaks To You*, wrote, "…the minute you take your 'religion' seriously, you've got to be concerned about your fellow men…Since the 'gospel' is concerned not only with individuals, but with individuals in their social relationships, it must be relevant to the way people order their social relationships."

Our cities—Memphis and the countless others in which we have family, friends and conduct business—need us to seek out ways to further encourage peace where we live. Whether through our professions or through volunteerism, through our churches and on our block, we can have influence over a young person. We can also help someone who may need our assistance, and find ways we can change our environment, either by cleaning up our surroundings, or addressing some of the challenges we find there.

Here is a simple way to remember this truth. You are at home, where you reside with at least two other people—could be you, a spouse and a teenager. A refrigerator stocked with food sits next to the stove, and its dinnertime. Everyone is hungry, yet no meal has been prepared. What should you do? The problem as it currently exists shows us that everyone has an appetite, and the resources to satisfy it are readily available, yet no one wants to cook. And then we wonder why we starve.

You Better Vote, and a Black Pastor is Saying this to You!!!! September 23, 2012

The New York *Daily News,* in an article dated September 17, 2012 presented a conversation many of us thought we would never hear in our lifetimes. In the article, "African-American Christians Waver Over Vote," the secondary caption reads, "Some black clergy say there is no good presidential choice between a Mormon candidate and one who supports gay marriage."[1] We go on to read that some black clergy are encouraging their congregants not to vote. NOT TO VOTE? Saying this in the very place that gave great assistance to the move for our full franchise as a people? DON'T VOTE? After the lives of many deacons, trustees, choir members, children and pastors have been given for us to be able to vote, you want to disgrace their memory and sacrifice, and give it away?

We see this development in the Church because we have allowed the Church to lose its way. When you set up a "name it and claim it, blab it and have it" theology, a relinquishing of looking at earthly reality while only looking toward heaven is all you will see. Out of this, we miss that God calls the church to be salt and light in the world, and that this life transformation takes place through a relationship with Jesus Christ, not legislated morality. When you vote for a president, you don't vote for him to become your pastor or church member, but you vote based on policies and how they affect the greater good. If you withhold your vote because the president embraces certain "sinners", what should you do with the rest of the "sinners" left in the church? Just asking…

If you really understand Scripture, it encourages us to have concern about the community in which we live. In Jeremiah 29, the Jews received encouragement to seek the peace with those in Babylon among whom they lived. In Luke 15, Jesus connects with those found on the margins, encouraging their reconnection with the community. These and other passages show us that Christians must be involved in shaping the good in their neighborhood, and voting is a way to ensure that this happens. Politicians shape laws that control the forward movement in a jurisdiction; the voter ensures that this happens in ways he or she supports. This is why voting is so important, and this is why for years many Black Americans were prevented from exercising this right. To consistently vote is a way to control your destiny. Not voting is actually a passive way of voting, and you may get what you don't want.

Don't listen to those with agendas and misguided applications of their faith stance; but every chance you get, after educating yourself on the issues, vote. That's the bottom line.

CHAPTER TWELVE - MISCELLANEOUS: THE PARKING LOT

How Times have Changed
Individualism vs. Community
Graduations in the Key of Life
It is Here
Will America ever "Come to Itself?"
Why Ban what so Many Want?
The Cult of Personality
Something I have to "Get Off My Chest"
A View on the Demise of Osama Bin Laden
Booker T. Washington High School and the President
We are All in the Same House
And a Child Shall Lead Them

How Times have Changed
July 12, 1998

As I prepared to write this message for today, I thought about what is taking place while you read this. Today is the completion of a pulpit swap begun back in May during our Senior Citizens Day. As you remember, Rev. David Fikes, pastor of Grace-St. Luke Episcopal Church, preached during our morning worship as part of MIFA's (Metropolitan Inter-Faith Association) "Faith- in–action" weekend. I was present for our celebration of Senior Citizens Day, and I am with the good people of Grace-St. Luke today as a representative of the greatest church in the created order.

The reality of where I am preaching today has become a ho-hum matter. There will probably be no news cameras there, no committee of "concerned members" meeting me at the front door, encouraging me to preach elsewhere. There will be no repercussions meted out to my family because of today's action. If the truth be told, I already know one or two of the members of that church, so it will be more of a feeling of being in familiar waters than of visiting.

This reality indicated that within many of our lifetimes, we have come a long way. God, through the vehicle of the Church, is to thank for this development. The Civil Rights Movement, as you know, was built in the crucible of the African-American experience with the Church as its launching pad. However, the work is not done. We still face great challenges in our city and country. The blood of

James Byrd in Texas and the gentleman who was set on fire in Virginia, among countless others, remind us that there is still work to do. The Hate Crimes Prevention Act of 1998 is designed to be just one vehicle to be used in addressing the present climate of our country.

I am convinced that Memphis will play a unique role in the healing of our nation, and perhaps we live for "such a time as this." Listen to the following description of our area from the Shelby County webpage:

> No other county in the United States has shaped American society more than Shelby County, Tennessee. Through our role in creating American's most distinctive music to transforming American business, Shelby County has changed the way that people around the world work and play. Like few places on the entire planet, Shelby County has been the seedbed for a creative energy that has given the world the blues, rockabilly, rock and roll, soul and the Memphis sound. Meanwhile, the business community has seen similar creativity that created a rich entrepreneurship that produced the world's first self-service grocery store, the world's first dime store, the world's first motel, the world's first drive-in restaurant, and the world's first overnight package delivery company.

I pray that a few short years from now we will live and mingle with all of our neighbors in ways beyond our wildest dreams. In doing so, we will cause God to smile.

Individualism vs. Community
June 11, 2000

About two Sundays ago, during Missionary Day, we had a minor mishap in our basement. As you know, mishaps take place from time to time, and this particular day was no exception. Water began to flow out of the men's restroom into the corridors and toward the fellowship hall. It was two inches deep in some places. This flow caused us to alter our reception location and created extra work for our custodian. The interesting thing about this mishap is that it could have been avoided. There was an "out of order" sign placed on the door of the downstairs men's restroom. However, someone, in their wisdom, decided that this sign was not for them. Because of that wise decision, many were inconvenienced, and the billfold of the church is a tad lighter.

It seems that more and more, individualism is the rule rather than the exception. Even in the life of the church, many seem to major in self-serving religion that regards God as a celestial bellhop. Everyone wants to be the boss; no one wants to be a worker. But a church centered on bosses without workers is not healthy and will not last. It won't grow, because people are not attracted to a setting where they have no input and everyone around them is a boss. God has designed the Church so that we cannot function without everyone working together for the common good.

As you consider your individual role and how it contributes to the whole of your church, keep in mind what Paul says about the reality of where our thinking and actions should be in 1 Corinthians 12:14-26: *Now the body is not made up of one part but of many. If the foot should say, 'Because I am not a hand, I do not belong to the body,' it would not for that reason cease to be part of the body. And if the ear should say, 'Because I am not an eye, I do not belong to the body,' it would not for that reason cease to be part of the body. If the whole body were an eye, where would the sense of hearing be? If the whole body were an ear, where would the sense of smell be? But in fact God has arranged the parts in the body, every one of them, just as he wanted them to be. If they were all one part, where would the body be? As it is, there are many parts, but one body. The eye cannot say to the hand, "I don't need you!" And the head cannot say to the feet, "I don't need you!" On the contrary, those parts of the body that seem to be weaker are indispensable, and the parts that we think are less honorable we treat with special honor. And the parts that are unpresentable are treated with special modesty, while our presentable parts need no special treatment. But God has combined the members of the body and has given greater honor to the parts that lacked it, so that there should be no division in the body, but that its parts should have equal concern for each other. If one part suffers, every part suffers with it; if one part is honored, every part rejoices with it.*

Graduations in the Key of Life
June 3, 2001

Today is Graduates Day at First Baptist. It is a day when we pause to recognize the educational advancement of our members. Our recognition of our graduates is important. There was a time in our collective past when it was illegal for our people to read, and those found guilty of empowering us in this way were severely punished. After slavery, schools and colleges were formed with the express purpose of empowerment through education. It is fitting that we honor our graduates today for there is, as Hebrews 12:1 states, *a great cloud of witnesses* who sit on the ramparts of glory, cheering us on. As they view us, they realize, as Hebrews 11:40 says, *God had planned something better for us so that only together with us would they be made perfect.*

If we take time to ponder, we begin to realize that life itself is a series of graduations. We move from humble beginnings to marginal progress, and then great success. We shift from limited shoe leather to an old, used car held together with nothing more than hope; then eventually we begin to drive reliable and stylish transportation. We go from a house with limited marketability and window fans to an exclusive neighborhood and central air.

Life presents us with loneliness, sickness and distress, and it does not allow us to ignore or walk around them. Each of us needs a source of sustenance to help us deal with these issues. Life mirrors in a profound way the Christian walk. If you have a relationship with Jesus Christ, it is an overriding assumption that you will grow spiritually. When a person does not grow, they stagnate. It's similar to putting money under a mattress instead of in a financial institution. Although the money itself is intact, its value erodes over time. All of us should evaluate today where we are with God. Perhaps it is time to admit that we have been like stagnant water and stand in need of being refreshed. God stands ready like the father of the prodigal son, to reactivate our fellowship with Him. With this reactivation comes a graduation through the school of experience to a sweet song due to the victory and redemption given by God.

It is Here
March 23, 2003

The anticipation hung in the air for months, similar to the climate in this city before the Tyson-Lewis fight. How will this event impact our city? Our lives? The war is here, and during the next few days, weeks, and months we will come to know what it will mean to us. At the beginning of this week, President Bush gave Saddam Hussein 48 hours to leave his country, speaking to him in a way reminiscent of the "stay in your place" conversations targeted toward African-Americans a generation ago. In light of this, the response was predictable. Over the past few years our foreign policy has helped, in large measure, to create this mess. Once upon a time Saddam Hussein and Osama bin Laden were our allies; now they are targets for elimination.

At the end of World War II, the Marshall Plan rebuilt Europe and Japan. This same type of spirit is needed to affect many of the nations of the world. What does Christian compassion look like? It should be concerned for the least of these. If we are truly a Christian nation, our foreign and national policies would reflect it. The world is jealous of our wealth. Can we share it without using the tools of exploitation?

Regardless of how we may feel about the war, let us remember our Armed Forces and their families. The personal interconnections of those left behind while we bear arms are the true face of war's impact.

Our sermon series dealing with the seven churches of Asia Minor remind us that regardless of the power of any nation, God is ultimately in control. During the time when Revelation was written, it appeared that the Roman Empire was invincible. Today it is merely the subject of history books. The opening volleys of this war may have brought us closer to the time when we experience the same fate. Jesus, however, lives forever and navigates His own away from the second death. Let us remember to anchor in Him.

Will America ever "Come to Itself?"
February 29, 2004

Luke 15:14-17: *After he had spent everything, there was a severe famine in that whole country, and he began to be in need. So he went and hired himself out to a citizen of that country, who sent him to his fields to feed pigs. He longed to fill his stomach with the pods that the pigs were eating, but no one gave him anything. When he came to his senses, he said, 'How many of my father's hired men have food to spare, and here I am starving to death!"*

Today's focus is on the prodigal, or lost and found, son. After he lost everything, he spent a period of time in the pigpen. We can come to this conclusion based on the language of the above text in verses 15 and 16. The text also implies that this son had become used to the pigs, an animal that as a good Jew he was to stay away from. He was around them every day because of his job description, becoming so comfortable in his surroundings that he was about to eat some of pigs' food in his hungered state. This son would've remained at the same job if his eyes hadn't been opened and he hadn't "come to his senses." After he woke up, he decided to go back to where he should have been all along.

We have become used to debauchery and desensitized to filth. Whether we say we belong to Christ or walk under another banner, there is within most of us a level of tolerance to all that is around us. For example, many were in uproar over what Janet Jackson did at this year's Super Bowl in exposing part of herself. Yet, the commercials during the telecast in many ways were just as bad, and the soap operas broadcast during that same week were probably just as risqué. To be fair, it was not a wise decision on Ms. Jackson's part, but perhaps we were upset because we witnessed impromptu instead of controlled debauchery.

> ***As we speak, gay and lesbian couples are flocking to San Francisco from across the nation to get married. President Bush, instead of finding the alleged weapons of mass destruction or providing a healing balm to the economy, wants a constitutional amendment to address the subject of gay marriage. A day after his public proclamation on this issue, the nation is told that adjustments will have to be made to Social Security so the money won't run out. When you couple this with questions about foreign policy and the war in Iraq, this administration begins to feel like the three card monty games of my youth down by the subway station. You get the illusion of victory yet you are quickly separated from your money.***

We affirm those relationships that connect with our pet sins and persecute others. These actions are part of the pot of filth. We live under an administration that positions its goals at the expense of others, yet we either can't see it or are too caught up in our own situations to care. Some presently complain about the violence in *The Passion of the Christ*, the new movie directed by Mel Gibson, which merely presents in a real way the harm done to Jesus as portrayed in the Gospels. Yet horror movies and gratuitous violence is fine, while the truth is not. It is time for us to focus on a return to God. This focus must begin on an individual basis. I encourage you during this season of Lent to take an introspective look, and as you change, your influence will begin to change others. God awaits anyone in the pigpen of society who, when looking at their circumstances, "comes to themselves."

Why Ban what so Many Want?
December 5, 2004

(This piece was in the "Viewpoint" section of the *Commercial Appeal*, while Dr. Hutchinson also served as the Chaplain of LeMoyne-Owen College)

Experts have critiqued it. Teachers have opinions about it. Parents have been for and against it. There is probably no one in this community who doesn't have a definite thought about it.

The issue of paddling in Memphis City Schools came to a resolution last month when the school board voted to remove corporal punishment from schools starting next fall. This issue, then, is over. Or is it?

Memphis City Schools are 87 % African-American. Based on recent surveys, and weighing general commentary from the community, it is safe to say that a good number of African-Americans wholeheartedly support corporal punishment. Many whom I have spoken with in churches, schools, barbershops, supermarkets and other places were disappointed with the board's vote. This sentiment runs contrary to that of many experts who cite the detrimental and ineffective aspects of paddling. It may be easy to say, "The vote has been taken, so let's move on." However, it's not quite that simple. Whenever you have a situation where people representing 87% of your clientele disagree in principle with a decision, the root causes of the disconnect should be examined.

I believe there are several reasons why we find great

support in the African-American community for paddling. The first is found in the teachings of the African-American church. From the earliest days of our nation, the church was fragmented sociologically on the basis of race, and the church in the black community became a source of strength, sustenance and direction. One of its principal teachings deals with the training of children.

Scripture verses such as *Train up a child in the way he should go: and when he is old, he will not depart from it* (Proverbs 22:6 KJV), and sayings such as "Spare the rod, spoil the child," resonate with many African-Americans and seem to be part of our DNA.

My 83-year-old mother, for example, lives by this credo. When I was growing up she had no problem applying the rod of correction to the seat of my understanding; many times, at the very scene of my transgression. The second reason is found partly in the realities of African-American life.

During the time of Jim Crow segregation, discipline was a necessary part of survival. To lead an undisciplined life in certain aspects could be disastrous. Discipline could be the difference between either an event-free day and life or "reckless eyeballing" and death. It was a way to ensure that lives and livelihoods would be preserved. Many a mother has told a son, "I'd rather whip you to keep the police from having to beat you."

After hearing some of the reasons why so many people affirm corporal punishment, we must now look at where we are. Paddling will be gone from our public-school system next fall. How should we proceed from here? Something is needed to curb the erosion of values and discipline in our schools. The suspension of an eighth-grade class at Geeter Middle School is an example of this need. That entire class was suspended after having a food fight that they would not clean up.

These challenges make the difficult job facing our public-school system even harder. Whether you are for or against corporal punishment, I'm sure you would agree that something must be done to make Memphis City Schools a better and safer learning environment for all students.
For me, the answer begins in the home. I reflect again on my 83-year-old mother. She practiced corporal punishment and much more. She made sure that I was exposed to the wider world at an early age through books and magazines. She set curfews and demanded discipline and respect.

I'm 6' 4" and look like a retired football player. My mother is 5' 6"; but you already know who was in charge. My mother never allowed me to run her house. She also lived in front of me the kind of life that she wanted to see from me. When I didn't get the message, privileges such as television and seeing friends were taken away. Corporal punishment was the last resort. My mother's method is a good example to follow. Parents and guardians – whether that's mother and father, a single mother, single father, grandmother, aunt, uncle or other adult – must show their children that they are loved. They must also seek out resources to help expand their children's horizons. There is no reason for a parent, coming to a school to hear why his child got suspended for participating in a food fight, to be placed in a squad car for disorderly conduct.

We must view our community as a village where everyone has a vested interest. Teachers must view every child as if they are his or her own. Those who are able can mentor and teach. Others can share resources. The village must raise those who have no model of excellence or nurturing atmosphere at home. Churches and various community centers are resources that can help with our children. Every one of us bears responsibility for making a difference that will ensure the ability of our youth to grow, learn and behave in Memphis City Schools.

The Cult of Personality
July 26, 2009

2 Kings 5:1-14, focus on vv. 1-3, 9-14: *Naaman, commander of the army of the king of Syria, was a great man with his master and in high favor, because by him the* L*ORD had given victory to Syria. He was a mighty man of valor, but he was a leper.* [2] *Now the Syrians on one of their raids had carried off a little maid from the land of Israel, and she waited on Naaman's wife.* [3] *She said to her mistress, "Would that my lord were with the prophet who is in Samaria! He would cure him of his leprosy."* [9] *So Naaman came with his horses and chariots, and halted at the door of Elisha's house.* [10] *And Elisha sent a messenger to him, saying, "Go and wash in the Jordan seven times, and your flesh shall be restored, and you shall be clean."* [11] *But Naaman was angry, and went away, saying, "Behold, I thought that he would surely come out to me, and stand, and call on the name of the* L*ORD his God, and wave his hand over the place, and cure the leper.* [12] *Are not Abana and Pharpar, the rivers of Damascus, better than all the waters of Israel? Could I not wash in them, and be clean?" So he turned and went away in a rage.* [13] *But his servants came near and said to him, "My father, if the prophet had commanded you to do some great thing, would you not have done it? How much rather, then, when he says to you, 'Wash, and be clean'?"* [14] *So he went down and dipped himself seven times in the Jordan, according to the word of the man of God; and his flesh was restored like the flesh of a little child, and he was clean* (RSV).

Today we have one national story that spawned two controversies. Professor Henry Louis "Skip" Gates, after getting past a stuck outside door, was removed from his own home in handcuffs after showing the appropriate ID. President Obama made remarks about this scenario, stating that the officers on the scene acted "stupidly" in their handling of this incident. We then hear how upstanding the arresting officer is, and African-American officers are found—including one who was at the scene—who support the actions of this officer. A rebuke concerning this issue is then leveled against the president.

The above example finds itself driven by something that is in the eyes of the beholder—style. It is, in some sense, anchored in the cult of personality. What is driving the Gates story is his prominence, his skin color, and a definite history of police subjectivity in this land and the ability of some to explain it away. We do it when friendship and family take precedence over right and wrong. We do it when personal convenience is more important than those around us, because they may not be like us.

In the text attached to my musing over this issue, Naaman was a leper, and was told by a nameless slave girl that a great prophet in Israel could heal him, and therefore make him socially acceptable and physically whole once again. Naaman eventually goes to Israel and shows up at the prophet's front door. The prophet sends word through his servant that Naaman should go to the Jordan River seven times and he would be whole. Naaman then was caught up in the cult of personality. He felt that since he "was somebody," the prophet should have the proper "style" and come out and greet him. Furthermore, he didn't want to dip in the muddy Mississippi, for if one wanted to be healed, this river didn't seem to be the place for it. The slave girl had to clear her throat and remind Naaman that if the prophet had said to do a great thing, would he not do it? So, brother leper, listen to the prophet and be made whole.

Don't get upset about seemingly being disrespected in your own home. Remember how to bow and scrape. What is the proper compass for how we view these situations? When similar situations take place with similar dynamics, are they handled the same? The Naamanite authorities have a problem with being called out for an overzealous reaction to a man entering his own home. Some who anchor in this way of thinking even have a problem with *their* President speaking his mind. I dare say that if Professor Gates lacked his present prominence, the outcomes would be far different.

The cult of personality will tell you how to act, and when, and we will like your performance based on whether we like you. Is this how you act? Is this how you determine right from wrong? All of us view life through the filters of history and experience, but if you are trying to live a God pleasing life, you will try to look at the facts of a situation instead of just the players involved.

Something I have to Get Off my Chest
September 12, 2010

I am a part of a small, interesting and strange collegium of people who make a bodacious claim. Out of all of the people on earth, many better equipped for the task, the Divine spoke to *me* and enlisted me to be a mouthpiece; speaking on behalf of a holy God to sinful, imperfect people just like me. As a pastor, I claim every week to hear from God in a manner sufficient to give a group of people gathered in faith "a word from the Lord." When the world views me and others like me, and the fact that we take ancient texts and use them to speak for a Higher Power in a modern world, the perception of us is closer to that of dinosaurs of an era long past than of current and relevant heralds.

With some of this in mind I am always careful to critique other heralds, sometimes even when their faith stance differs from mine. I may take issue at times with a misuse of a particular text, and even sometimes pray for their motives, seen or unseen; but I always operate under the assumption that they at least made an attempt to hear from God before they speak to us. Therefore, as I now look at Gainesville, Florida, and the Reverend Terry Jones, who, as of this writing, is preparing to burn the Koran—Islam's Bible—on September 11, 2010, which is the 9-year anniversary of what happened in New York, Washington, and Pennsylvania, anger surfaces. This pastor has allegedly said that God is leading him to do this. Well, I must pull off the polite, Memphis exterior, temporarily suspend proper English, excuse decorum, and revisit my hometown—The Bronx—to say this to this pastor:

QUIT LYING ON GOD!!!!

This must be the God who caused some people to use fire hoses on other people instead of buildings. Those who serve this kind of God are people who could own slaves and yet send missionaries to Africa; people who pillage and fleece the flock. In other words, these are church folk—not Christians—but people who occupy pews but don't know Jesus. Because of Pastor Jones' insanity, tensions all over the world are heightened, and the only one happy is Satan.

In closing, let me suggest how you may want to approach this issue. Yes, each of us can make a difference. We can live our relationship with Jesus in such a way that others can see true Christianity in action. While doing this we recognize that God gives us choice whether we commit to Jesus Christ or not. *…behold I stand at the door and knock…* (Revelation 3:20 KJV) are the words of Jesus. Live in such a way for Jesus that the world sees Him in you. That is a far more intelligent and effective witness than burning books, and instead of lying on God you will truly be representing the Divine.

A View on the Demise of Osama Bin Laden
May 8, 2011

As a native New Yorker, I have for almost the past 30 years driven over the world-famous Brooklyn Bridge, looking at the skyline of lower Manhattan before turning onto the FDR Drive. This trip, begun in earlier years out of necessity, has now become a ritual every time I have the opportunity to visit my home town. I still remember the first time I took this route, looking up and seeing the World Trade Center. As a dyed in the wool urbanite, this very location, on the bridge looking up, has given me great peace across the years. It was the intersection of God-given knowledge being applied through the old (the bridge) and the fairly new skyscraper constructed when I was a child. As I write this, I remember the Twin Towers with the two floors of shopping, the subway, a PATH station taking commuters to New Jersey, and the constant press of multicolored humanity that moved below, around, through, and in these buildings.

And then September 11, 2001 changed my favorite view, the New York skyline, and the collective psyche of New Yorkers and all Americans. I called The Bronx to check on childhood friends, and accidently dialed the number of a firehouse in my old neighborhood. The fireman on the other end of the line told me that the smell of Ground Zero had made its way to the firehouse, about 20 miles away.

Last Sunday, about 10:30 p.m. our time, celebration of the death of Osama bin Laden rang across this country. Since then, there have been many who have said that to celebrate the death of a man, albeit a wicked one, goes against the principles of people of faith. Others have rightly said that the terrorist threat still remains—and to look for its increase as a result of this action. To me, the celebration for many isn't blood thirst, but psychological closure. Until last Sunday, many Americans were like the victims of violent crimes, who, not receiving counseling, were left to battle their pain and suffering alone. Since 9/11, America fought, and still fights, in two wars, with the potential of a third. The bloodshed of our troops becomes more common. A country unaccustomed to defeat and abuse, until Sunday, was incomplete. Much more importantly, those who directly suffered as a result of these attacks, and then forgotten by the country, needed closure.

As people of faith, we know that life introduces us to suffering caused by the wicked. We must remind others and ourselves that wickedness did not cease on the earth due to the demise of bin Laden, just as it continued after the death of Adolph Hitler. As we live our faith, it is incumbent upon us to be a living epistle of how to live through our pain, of how to be wounded healers, and how to live as the righteous so that evil will be made to retreat. Light repels darkness, and whether it be the misguided burners of Korans, the birthers who major in the nonexistent, racists with a divisive agenda, or those who live in Christian religion rather than a relationship with Jesus Christ, we who know better must continue to be bright lights of the Lord's love.

Booker T. Washington High School and the President May 29, 2011

This past Monday ranks as one of the single most historic experiences in this city. The first Black President of the United States came to Memphis as the commencement speaker for Booker T. Washington High School. In his speech, President Obama shared with the graduates his personal challenges growing up in a single parent home, highlighting the role that education played in his life. His presence was an exciting, overwhelming journey for many of this year's graduates, for it signaled an occasion many thought they would never see.

Many people, being cynics, speak of the obvious fact that there were many who didn't know or care about the school before this graduation. Part of their critique stems from the fact that BTW is in one of the poorest zip codes in Memphis, and had received scant attention until now. They want to know if the bandwagon will roll away now that the graduation is over.

The cynical miss the larger point. Lives in 38126 and around Memphis will change because of President Obama's presence and words of encouragement. That alone is worth all of the attention. It will also encourage Principal Kiner and the staff of the school in moving forward with the work entrusted to them. It will also let Memphians look higher and think bigger than we have accustomed ourselves to.

The cynical will always be with us, but unlike those who labor and then get rewards, history doesn't remember their names. This should be a sign that our focus must always be to trust God and work as unto the Lord.

We are All in the Same House
January 29, 2012

As part of the "Faith in Memphis" panel for the *Commercial Appeal*, Memphis' major daily newspaper, I was asked to comment on the following:

> Several of our suburbs are taking steps to form their own school systems, in large part to avoid being part of the coming unified Shelby County school district. How do you feel about this? Should our suburbs form their own school systems? How might this help or hurt the community at large?

Here is my response:

1 Corinthians 11:17-22: *Now in the following instructions I do not commend you, because when you come together it is not for the better but for the worse.* [18] *For, to begin with, when you come together as a church, I hear that there are divisions among you; and to some extent I believe it.* [19] *Indeed, there have to be factions among you, for only so will it become clear who among you are genuine.* [20] *When you come together, it is not really to eat the Lord's supper.* [21] *For when the time comes to eat, each of you goes ahead with your own supper, and one goes hungry and another becomes drunk.* [22] *What! Do you not have homes to eat and drink in? Or do you show contempt for the church of God and humiliate those who have nothing? What should I say to you? Should I commend you? In this matter I do not commend you* (NRSV)*!*

Mark 3:25: *If a house is divided against itself, that house cannot stand.*

Fear.

It is worry and panic about the future.

Fear.

It is holding on to the past. It is believing in perceptions that have an ounce of truth and a pound of lies. It is what is driving, I believe, the insanity of the suburban towns moving with accelerated speed to form their own school systems. Of course, every municipality has the right to self-determination, so the question of whether our suburbs should form their own school systems, from that perspective, is a moot one. The real question is, "Should it happen?" Let me paraphrase the comedian Chris Rock for the answer, just because you can drive with your feet doesn't make it a good idea.

Why such a blunt, borderline crass answer? The two Scripture texts highlighted above—the first from Paul, the second from Jesus—share a similar sentiment with that blunt statement. The church in 1 Corinthians would gather for a memorial meal in conjunction with the Lord's Supper (this is Communion for some of you) and forget its intent. They wouldn't share the meal like we do in churches all over Memphis in our fellowship halls, but they would take what they brought and eat it among themselves. Those who couldn't or didn't bring anything were left out. The selfish, gluttonous individuals got drunk, and others went hungry. As you can see by the text, Paul was not pleased.

Jesus sums this up well by reminding us that a house divided against itself cannot stand.

Shelby County is a singular house. Memphis, Germantown, Bartlett, Lakeland, Collierville, Capelville, Arlington and Millington are rooms in this house. Wanting to separate before you even know what the process will do will divide the house. Viewing different sections of the house like the Hatfields and McCoys won't help either. Contrary to some opinions, people in South Memphis for the most part want better schools in their neighborhood. They have no desire to send their children 30 miles to school in Collierville, and if Collierville children were in a South Memphis classroom, those neighborhood parents would want to know why they were there. Both areas have a similar desire for having strong neighborhood schools that would negate the need for any sort of busing, and in that spirit, each room in the house should be in outstanding condition. We have the opportunity to shape a world-class school system that retains local control, but if the suburban towns remain intent on forming separate school districts, it won't happen.

The alternative is far worse. The effects won't happen right away, but eventually property values for the region will be undesirable. Why? Because the core city will be dead. It will be like a home that has a burned out kitchen and living room, but the residents of the home don't care because they have hot plates, refrigerators and televisions in their bedrooms. It is time for all of us in Shelby County to be selfish about the good for all. We will then see the nation coming to us for ideas, and we will cease to be at the bottom of all the good national lists, and at the top of the bad ones. Remember, a definition of insanity is doing the same thing over and over again and expecting different results. Setting up these individual school districts is the same thing we had this time last year.

My suburban brothers and sisters, I hope you will change your minds. However, if you don't care about unity, then move away like you threaten to. Set up school districts around Memphis that put us back to where we were over a year ago.

Or better yet…drive with your feet.

And a Child Shall Lead Them
September 16, 2012

Isaiah 11:6: *The wolf shall live with the lamb, the leopard shall lie down with the kid, the calf and the lion and the fatling together, and a little child shall lead them* (NRSV).

Mark 9:36-37: *Then he took a little child and put it among them; and taking it in his arms, he said to them, "Whoever welcomes one such child in my name welcomes me, and whoever welcomes me welcomes not me but the one who sent me* (NRSV).

This past Monday, students from George Washington Carver High School decided that they had enough. About 100 students said enough of no air conditioning in several parts of the school during the hottest month of the year; they said enough to scheduling problems that allegedly had some 9th graders with nothing on their schedules except lunch, and they said enough to the cuts affecting the choir and the band. These students, because of their grievances, executed a peaceful boycott of their school.

Some who read this may think these children ought to be in school. Others may not care. Still others, agreeing with some of the recommendations of recent reform educators, see no need for the arts in school—in spite of studies across the years that show their effectiveness in helping students become critical thinkers. It is interesting that issues such as the ones brought forth by these students seldom surface in schools other than those in inner cities across this nation. The students, realizing that they attend school in the "out of sight, out of mind" part of the district, took matters into their own hands.

What these students did reminds me of the power of youth. Historically, it is youth movements that bring positive change. A similar movement to this week's happened in 1976. At that time, students in the Black townships of South Africa recently began their classroom instruction in Afrikaans, which symbolized for the students the language of their oppressors, instead of English. On June 16, about 20,000 students protested these changes, and were attacked by the South African police. An estimated 700 students died in the ensuing violence, but this protest is what turned the tide of apartheid in the local and international community. We now have a democratic South Africa today in large part because of…schoolchildren.

God values children, so much so that in our first text they are the symbol of a new reality, and in the second, dear to God. Youth possess the ability to shift for good those things that are out of balance. My final word, then, is to our youth. The world awaits your direction and input. After learning from the past, chart your course. Its lessons give you the foundation for what you see today. Who knows, you might change a school system and a nation.

ACKNOWLEDGEMENTS

In this the "remix" of this work, I thank all of the residents of my village, with all of its subdivisions. I thank the New York village from The Bronx – my birthplace, to Brooklyn, New Rochelle and Hackensack, New Jersey; and all points in between. I thank the diaspora that is my family; from Jamaica to New York, New Jersey, Florida, Atlanta, Toronto, Cuba, London, Birmingham, England and Malaysia—and these are the places that we know about! There are a lot of us! Shout outs also to my Brandeis family, Drew Theological School family, Bronx Science family, and United Theological family. Last, but by no means least, the Memphis village, from the Soulsville community where I live, to LeMoyne Owen College, to all of the pastors, churches, and salt of the earth good folk; thanks for accepting me as a part of the village. Usually you're tough on outsiders, and native New Yorkers get no play (smile), but for some reason you've embraced me as your own, and even catch feelings when some of the New Yorkers try to claim me! I love you too.

I also thank "the cloud of witnesses" which include my parents, Noel G. L. Hutchinson, Sr., and Agnes D. Hutchinson, Reverend Richard C. Gay, Dr. Gardner C. Taylor, Dr. Charles L. Dinkins, Sr., my maternal grandmother Mabel Jones Hart, and a vast assemblage of persons known and unknown who have ever beseeched God on my behalf. I must acknowledge that I live a life kissed by God. As you have read in this book, I'm here because of answered prayers.

Let me also thank Latrivia Welch and RiverHouse Publishing for helping me bring the remix to life. A big thank you goes out to Donnetta Booker for the task of editing and proofreading this work, giving it a fresh set of purposeful eyes. I thank Dr. Cheryl Townsend Gilkes, a phenomenal intellect and writer in her own right. A big thank you also goes to Walter Fields of the *North Star News*, who has been a constant source of encouragement and help. I also must give a shout out to Dr. Frank Thomas, author and preacher extraordinaire, for his advice, encouragement, and council.

I also owe a big debt of gratitude to the churches that undoubtedly shaped my Christian foundation and witness. From my first church, St. Edmund's Episcopal Church in The Bronx, to Bethesda Baptist Church in New Rochelle, New York—pastored by my father in ministry, Dr. Allen Paul Weaver, Jr.—thank you for all you have done. To the Mount Olive Baptist Church in Hackensack, New Jersey, where I did my field ministry for Drew Seminary while serving as their first Youth Minister, bless and thank you; I especially thank and appreciate Dr. Gregory J. Jackson for all his support across the years.

I thank the Senior Pastor, Dr. Gary V. Simpson, and congregants of the great Concord Baptist Church in Brooklyn, New York. Thanks go out to the Progressive National Baptist Convention (PNBC), our President, Dr. James C. Perkins, and our General Secretary, Dr. Timothy T. Boddie, as well as the pastors and members of the Tennessee Progressive Baptist Council. I also thank the congregants of First Baptist Church Lauderdale in Memphis, Tennessee. You've seen my highs and lows as we have engaged in ministry together. Thank you for over 22 years in which we have grown in God's grace. I'm still just a phone call away.

I also thank all of those I've met during the course of hosting my TV show—Dr. Ivory Taylor, Eddie Jones, and Deidre Malone. A shout out goes to the Memphis Association of Black Journalists (MABJ), and all of the local television anchors in Memphis who offered words of support and encouragement. Special shout outs go to local TV anchors Stephanie Scurlock, April Thompson, and the late Ben Watson. To David Waters of *The Commercial Appeal*, thank you much.

To my wife Rebecca, thank you for your love, and the initial prodding and encouragement that brought this project to fruition. There is a well-worn saying, "Behind every great man is a great woman." I think that saying should be changed to, "*Beside* every great man is a *greater* woman." That's how I feel about you. Eyes have not seen what God will yet place in your hands. You are phenomenal.

As this is the remix, that means the music is still playing. It also means that more music, more lyrics, more singing is yet coming. Simply put, if I didn't call your name in these first two books, "keep hope alive." Don't be upset, your day is coming. The record is almost over...I appreciate all of you. Gotta go.

Peace.

About the Author

Dr. Noel G. L. Hutchinson, Jr. was recently named Mission Director for the Progressive National Baptist Convention (PNBC). He is also the organizer and founder of a new ministry, Greater Works Fellowship, and was the pastor of First Baptist Church Lauderdale in Memphis, Tennessee for 22 years. A native of The Bronx, New York, he obtained his Bachelor of Arts degree from Brandeis University in the areas of Sociology and American Studies, a Master of Divinity *cum laude* from Drew Theological School, and a Doctor of Ministry degree from United Theological Seminary in Trotwood, Ohio. Dr. Hutchinson served as an adjunct professor at Memphis Theological Seminary, and was the

College Chaplain at LeMoyne-Owen College, where under his leadership LeMoyne-Owen began a Faith in Action Community Conference in partnership with the Congress of National Black Churches, Memphis Affiliate. Dr. Hutchinson has preached nationally; and internationally in Guyana, South America; Montego Bay, Jamaica; Turin, Italy; and Cape Town, South Africa with the Lott Carey Baptist Foreign Mission Convention.

Dr. Hutchinson has also been active in various civic and community efforts. Some of his involvements include being a past president of the Memphis Ministers Association, and the current president of the Tennessee Progressive Baptist Council. He also has served on the following boards: the Memphis NAACP, Memphis Urban League, Church and Community Investment Fund, The Church Health Center, and the Metropolitan Interfaith Association (MIFA). He is also a 1997 graduate of *Leadership Memphis.* In November 2013, he became the host of "Black Thought," airing weekdays on MUTV1, now the M1 network, Memphis' first Black-owned television station.

Greater Works Fellowship is a new ministry in an embryonic, organizational stage theologically based on John 14:12, where Jesus said, *Very truly, I tell you, the one who believes in me will also do the works that I do and, in fact, will do greater works than these* (NRSV). Much of this book embodies the three focus areas of GWF—impact, empowerment, and witness, showing in practical ways how a Christian should fully be a positive change agent, while engaging the world around him/her. Simply put, we hope to develop Christians who fully interact as catalysts wherever they are in the world.

For more information, go to greatworksmemphis.com

END NOTES TO FOLLOW

---

[i] *Robert McAfee Brown, The Bible Speaks To You, Westminster John Knox, 1985, pg. 286*

[ii] *Schube, Sam, GQ magazine December 14, 2017, "Gucci and Dapper Dan Are Officially in Business"*

[iii] *ibid, Brown*

[iv] *Neil A. Lewis, in The New York Times "President Faults Race Preferences as Admission Tool"*
http://www.nytimes.com/2003/01/16/national/16AFFI.html?module=Search&mabReward=relbias%3Ar

[v] *Mike Allen and Charles Lane, in The Washington Post, "Rice Helped Shape Bush Decision on Admissions", January 17, 2003, pg. A.01, A Section*

[vi] *Fred A. Bernstein, in The New York Times "Derrick Bell, Law Professor and Rights Advocate, Dies at 80"*
http://www.nytimes.com/2011/10/06/us/derrick-bell-pioneering-harvard-law-professor-dies-at-80.html?pagewanted=all&module=Search&mabReward=relbias%3Ar%2C%5B%22RI%3A5%22%2C%22RI%3A15%22%5D&_r=0

[vii] *Greg Garrison, in al.com "Fred Shuttlesworth, Birmingham civil rights legend, dies at 89"*
http://blog.al.com/spotnews/2011/10/fred_shuttlesworth_obituary.html

[viii] *Tutu, Desmond, No Future Without Forgiveness, Doubleday, New York, 1999, pg. 31*

8 *Angus MacSwain, for Reuters "It is an Ideal for which I am Prepared to Die," December 5, 2013* http://www.reuters.com/article/2013/12/05/us-mandela-speech-idUSBRE9B419620131205

9 *YouTube video excerpt of an interview with Nelson Mandela* https://www.youtube.com/watch?v=HED4h00xPPA

10 *Detroit Free Press, "Affirmative Action Case Expected to Reach High Court," May 16, 2002, pg. B.1, Section NWS*

xi *The hero's journey : Joseph Campbell on his life and work, the world of Joseph Campbell / edited and with an introduction by Phil Cousineau ; foreword by Stuart L. Brown, executive editor. Campbell, Joseph San Francisco : Harper & Row, c1990. pg xxiv*

12 *Detroit Free Press, "Affirmative Action Case Expected to Reach High Court," May 16, 2002, pg. B.1, Section NWS*

xiii *The Council produced a commercial that ran on local stations for two weeks in 2016. It was followed by appearances on local TV shows. The following was an unsolicited comment on Facebook from a viewer who saw one of these broadcasts:* Christian Kirk September 4, 2016 ·

I am so proud to have turned on the television this morning to WMC 5 to see the history being made before my eyes. My dear friends, Dr. Noel Hutchinson *and*

Dr. Andre Johnson were joined by their colleagues in the Tennessee Progressive Baptist Council to denounce police brutality. When was the last time you've seen this bravery and awareness from the ministers in Memphis? This is #TheMovement. What did your preacher do this morn-

ing? #SpeakUp#HeCameToSetTheCaptivesFree #YourPreacherShouldBePreachingFreedom

[xiv] *TV commercial that ran in Memphis: https://www.facebook.com/TennesseeProgressiveBaptistCouncil/videos/331593080551940/*

[xv] *On WATN –TV Memphis. Pastor Says Presence of Police TACT Unit At Peaceful Event Was Insensitive. localmemphis.com*

http://www.localmemphis.com/news/local-news/pastor-says-presence-of-police-tact-unit-at-peaceful-event-was-insensitive/781722462

[xvi] *https://natw.org/about*

[xvii] *This was originally posted on Facebook, and made into a Shepherd's Staff entry for the next Sunday*

[xviii] *David Waters, opinion/engagement editor of the Commercial Appeal, Memphis' daily newspaper, read this, and asked me to do an op-ed piece. It is the next entry*

[xix] *Keep in mind that the newspaper provides the caption. This one is not mine—but theirs! Note that it varies from the Facebook post because it targets a wider, slightly different audience.*

[xx] *This post generated responses from administrators of the National Civil Rights Museum, and private conversations with present and former elected officials.*

[xxi] *This was the speech given by President Trump (that was hard to write!) at the opening of the Mississippi Civil Rights Museum*

[xxii] *A part of 1 John 4:4*

[xxiii] *This post generated much conversation, and sparked some rekindled development here in Memphis*

[xxiv] *This post was prompted by the sudden death of Bernal Smith, Jr., publisher of the Tri-State Defender, Memphis' Black owned newspaper. John Best is the Broadcast Operations Advisor for the Department of Broadcast Services for Shelby County Schools (SCS). He also hosts a radio show on 88.5 FM, the FM station for SCS.*

[xxv] *A part of Proverbs 6:19*

[xxvi] *From the NFL game operations manual: "During the National Anthem, players on the field and bench area should stand at attention, face the flag, hold helmets in their left hand, and*

*refrain from talking."*https://www.si.com/nfl/2017/09/25/does-nfl-require-players-stand-national-anthem

xxvii *From the song "Wake Up Everybody" written by John Whitehead, Gene McFadden, and Victor Carstarphen, and sung by Harold Melvin and the Blue Notes, with Teddy Pendergrass singing lead*

xxviii *reference to "Keep On Truckin," written by Leonard Caston, Jr, Anita Poree, and Frank Wilson, sung by Eddie Kendricks*

xxix *On July 17, 2015, Darrius Stewart, a 19 year old Black man, was killed by a Memphis police officer. He was a passenger in a cart stopped for a broken taillight. Due to the nature of this case, it garnered much attention. Here is some information:*
http://www.wmcactionnews5.com/story/29578116/man-dead-after-struggle-with-mpd-officer

The Tennessee Bureau of Investigation (TBI) documents on the case:
https://www.dropbox.com/sh/ze8wukis3wkltxe/AADqP3L9Uejn9sNSe1D6E34sa?dl=0

xxx *The Shelby County grand jury, after a unicorn rare indictment of a police officer by the DA, decided that this case shouldn't be tried. At a press conference that was held outside 201 Poplar (our jail/court complex), one Black clergy person pleaded for calm. After he spoke, this is what I said: "Something smells bad with our justice system. Yes we sh*ould remain calm but that

doesn't mean we're going to remain silent. Yes we should remain calm, but that doesn't mean we won't be strategic. And yes we should remain calm but that doesn't mean we won't act." Several others both commented, responded, and reminded me of what I said.

[xxxi] *YouTube video https://www.youtube.com/watch?v=GlKL_EpnSp8 done by Bomani Armah*

[xxxii] *example of online Bible study https://www.youtube.com/watch?v=pSPuABMS36M&t=304s*

[xxxiii] *"Lift Him Up," written by Johnson Oatman, Jr and Benjamin B. Beall*

[34] *Jeff Jacoby, in the Boston Globe, "A cardinal's compassion for a killer" (original article for "Compassion for a Cold-blooded Killer" in the Commercial Appeal), September 24, 1996, pg. 1, Section A17*

[xxxv] *Nicholas Kristof, "And Jesus Said Unto Paul of Ryan ..." in The New York Times March 16, 2017*

[xxxvi] *http://www.music-lyrics-gospel.com/gospel_music_lyrics/only_what_you_do_for_christ_will_last_1056.asp*

---

xxxvii http://www.nba.com/cavaliers/news/gilbert_letter_100708.html

xxxviii *Arlene Levinson, in the Associated Press, "Grotesque Murder Is Investigated for Racial Motives" August 17, 1997* http://articles.latimes.com/1997/aug/17/news/mn-23228

xxxix *Lubbock Avalanche-Journal lubbockonline.com, "Suspect's racist tattoos shown to Jasper jurors", February 18, 1999,* http://lubbockonline.com/stories/021899/sta_021899076.shtml

xl *Claude Sitton, Special to the New York Times, "Negro Sitdowns Stir Fear Of Wider Unrest in South", February 14, 1960, pg. 1, Section 1*

xli *ibid*

xlii *http://www.music-lyrics-gospel.com/gospel_music_lyrics/life_every_voice_and_sing_3704.asp*

xliii *Foster, Richard, The Celebration of Discipline, Harper San Francisco, 1998, pg. 32*

xliv *http://www.gpo.gov/fdsys/pkg/BILLS-105hr3330ih/pdf/BILLS-105hr3330ih.pdf*

[xlv] *Keller, Timothy, The Reason for God, Dutton, New York, 2008, pg. 26*

[xlvi]

https://ncadv.org/assets/2497/domestic_violence.pdf

[xlvii] *McCall, Nathan, Makes Me Wanna Holler, Random House, New York, 1994, pp. 115, 117, 139*

[xlviii] *Geoff Calkins, in the Commercial Appeal, "Nothing Memphis Can't Do", May 1, 2002, pg. D1, Sports Section*

[xlix] http://www.cyclopaedia.info/wiki/G.-A.-Studdert-Kennedy-1

[l] *Associated Press, September 17, 2012, as found in the New York Daily News, "African-American Christians waver over vote" http://www.nydailynews.com/news/politics/african-american-christians-waver-vote-article-1.1161290*

www.ingramcontent.com/pod-product-compliance
Lightning Source LLC
Chambersburg PA
CBHW031041110426
42740CB00047B/777

9780998810867